FOURTEEN EIGHTEEN

FOURTEEN EIGHTEEN

John Masters

TRANSWORLD PUBLISHERS LIMITED
A NATIONAL GENERAL COMPANY

FOURTEEN EIGHTEEN

A CORGI BOOK 552 98558 9

Originally published in Great Britain
by Michael Joseph Limited

PRINTING HISTORY
Michael Joseph edition published 1965
Corgi edition published 1970

Copyright © 1965 Bengal-Rockland Inc.

This book is set in 11pt Plantin Series 110

Corgi Books are published by
Transworld Publishers Ltd.,
Cavendish House, 57–59, Uxbridge Road,
Ealing, London, W.5
Printed in Great Britain by
Fletcher & Son Ltd., Norwich

For Ethel Allcard

ACKNOWLEDGEMENTS

Most of the substance of this book appeared, in different form, in the *News of the World* during July, August and September of 1964, in commemoration of the fiftieth anniversary of the outbreak of the Great War. My thanks are due to that newspaper and to C. J. Lear and John Jarrett for their help in casting and editing the original articles. Many people helped by talking to me about their experiences in the Great War, and by allowing me access to their private papers; their names appear throughout the text, and I thank them all.

The selection of the photographs to go with the text would have been impossible without the unstinted co-operation of the staff of the Imperial War Museum, particularly Mr Edward Hine and the Photographic Librarian, Mr J. F. Golding. Textual research was much smoothed by the helpfulness of Mr Peter Simkins, of the Imperial War Museum's Department of Research and Publications. My thanks are also due to Mr Ed Rollins of the B.B.C.

I record my appreciation of Messrs Michael Joseph's generosity in releasing Miss Judith McAlister of their editorial staff to work with me on this project. Public appreciation is due to Miss McAlister herself for a task done cheerfully, carefully, and well – a task that continued, incidentally, long after my own work was done.

JOHN MASTERS

My thanks are due to Heinemann & Co. Ltd for permission to quote from *History of 60 Squadron, R.A.F.* by Group-Capt. A. J. L. Scott; to Her Majesty's Stationery Office for permission to quote from *The War in the Air* by H. A. Jones, published by Oxford University Press; to Sifton Praed & Co. Ltd for permission to quote from *A History of the 2nd Lancers (Gardner's Horse) from 1809 to 1922* by D. E. Whitworth, M.C.; to Geoffrey Bles Ltd for permission to quote from *Fortune Grass* by Mabel Lethbridge, and to Mrs E. M. Bilbrough for permission to quote from Mrs Bilbrough's Diary.

Other books which I have found valuable and which might interest readers are: *Years of Combat* by Sholto Douglas (Collins, 1963); *Invisible Weapons* by J. C. Silber (Hutchinson, 1932); *In the Hands of Senoussi* by Capt. Gwatkin Williams, R.N. (C. Arthur Pearson Ltd, 1916); *Hell at Ypres* by John T. Hunter (The Naylor Co., San Antonio, Texas, 1934); *War is War* by ex-Private X (A. McLelland Burrage) (Gollancz, 1930); *A Subaltern's War* by Charles Edmonds (C. E. Carrington) (Peter Davies, 1929); *At G.H.Q.* by Brig.-Gen. John Charteris (Cassell, 1931); *Vain Glory* by Guy Chapman (Cassell, 1937); and *Allenby, Soldier and Statesman* by Lord Wavell (Harrap, 1946).

The pre-war Army: Royal Progress through the City of London, 1911
(by courtesy of Radio Times Hulton Picture Library)

PREFACE

The war of 1914–18 is sometimes called the First World War and sometimes the Great War. The second is the proper title, for it was a turning point of history. The Second World War, and the Cold War, are only the heavings of the troubled earth as it tries to make a stable pattern out of the new emotions, new conditions, and new organisms thrown up by the Great War.

The Great War is not "great" because it caused the death of so many million men and women, the ruin of so many million houses, churches, banks, ships, post offices, railway locomotives. The scope of its destructiveness was indeed unequalled, but only because in previous time mankind did not possess the tools for mechanized savagery on such a scale. If he had, he would certainly have used them, and with no less determined a ferocity, as the briefest look at the Thirty Years War will attest. The 1914–18 war earns its sobriquet in the same way that the French Revolution does, but with even clearer title.

Nothing was the same afterwards as before. The French Revolution destroyed a social system that had flourished in Europe for almost a thousand years: the Great War destroyed Europe itself. The French Revolution destroyed faith in Church and Sovereign: the Great War destroyed faith in God and Man. From the French Revolution came social doctrines founded in a belief in human teachability, belief in the value of the individual, confidence of man's inherent nobility. From the Great War came political doctrines founded in belief in man's inherent brutality, in his fears and hates, in confidence of his individual un-importance.

It is not my intention to write a history of this mighty event, or of any particular part of it. Many such have been written, and most of the recent ones have been very good. What I am trying to do is cast a personal, emotional and wandering light on the war. So might a lighthouse, its beam revolving in the dusk, reveal fitful glimpses of a great, battered warship as it drifts away and into the past – now shining on the troubled faces of the officers on the bridge; now on a group of sailors on the deck, some singing, some crying, some bleeding; now on the long guns, smoke from the last of those salvoes which destroyed a continent and reshaped a world still drifting from the muzzles . . .

I have selected six moments on which to focus my light: the battles of Mons and Le Cateau – because they were the beginning, and because they were the only ones fought by the old Regular Army: the battles of Coronel and the Falkland Islands, together with the subsequent sinking of the *Dresden* – because they form a drama of classical Greek form and dimension: the War in the Air – because it was the first, and because it gave birth to modern knights and rebirth to ancient chivalry: the battle of Passchendaele – for its utter, useless, heroic stupidity, epitome of the stupidity and heroism that marked, respectively, the highest leaders and the lowliest led in the war as a whole: the Zeebrugge raid of St George's Day, 1918 – because it was a commando expedition and a wonderful piece of derring-do, a flash of the Drake spirit in a Navy suffering from too much weight and too little imagination: and the battle of Armageddon – because it was the last great horsed cavalry action in history, and because it was a lesson in the art of generalship, and a mighty victory.

Between the longer looks at these large-scale events we shall take brief glances at a few scenes on the flank and rear of the main struggle. And we shall hear, in snatches, like the words of someone passing and repassing our window, the authentic voice of the England of those days. These – the short pieces printed in italics – are excerpts from the war diary of Mrs Ethel M. Bilbrough, of Chisle-hurst.

Let us imagine it is turning dark outside our lighthouse, then. A storm is rising, a great storm, a mighty, terrifying storm. It is time to turn on the light . . .

MONS AND LE CATEAU

August 23, 1914, and one name, a single syllable, tolls for all of island birth: *Mons!* The bell for the end of an era, the beginning of a long agony, a longer austerity: *Mons!*

It is a mining town, gaunt and dirty, with brick houses and smoking slag-heaps. The British Army had fought little in towns. Its experience was on the African veldt, the Indian Frontier mountains, the Burmese rice paddy; but the men standing behind the angles of the walls, rifles negligently ready, were not over-awed. It had been a long wait, but the time was very close now, this Sunday morning with the church bells calling the people to Mass.

Officers strolled from post to post, checking positions, exchanging quiet words. Two men came up from the rear, one wiping the back of his hand appreciatively across his mouth. "A drop of char's just the thing before a scrap," he said.

"*Teek hai*, Bill," the other answered.

It was warm, this year of the magic, burning summer, but there had been ground mist since first light and now a light summer rain fell.

Perhaps they would hear the hoof-beats first. Or would the mist and the rain deaden sounds, so that they'd *see* before they heard, the flat-topped mortar-board sort of hats, and the lance points, glittering?

A private of the 4th Middlesex took his pipe from his mouth – "Here they come."

14

The platoon officer looked, and nodded. They all waited, holding back under the walls until the Germans came closer. Then the rifles fired, a short vicious crackle. The battle of Mons had begun.

The British Expeditionary Force held the line of the Mons Canal, which runs straight east and west. Farthest on the right stood the Royal Scots; very properly, for this is the Royal Regiment, the 1st Foot. Then came the Gordon Highlanders; then the Royal Irish, Middlesex, Royal Fusiliers, Royal Scots Fusiliers, Northumberland Fusiliers, Royal West Kents, King's Own Scottish Borderers, East Surreys, Duke of Cornwall's Light Infantry . . . They spoke in the accents of every county, every city, but they shared a common past and a common way of thought and action, for these were the regulars of the old line. Here, along the canal, they all belonged to the 3rd and 5th Divisions of General Smith-Dorrien's II Corps.

The Germans came on, marching in mass down the road towards the canal bridges at Obourg and Nimy, singing their march songs. Six divisions of them faced the two British. The Germans wore field-grey uniforms, jackboots, and black helmets with tall spikes, but the helmet and its ornate front badge were hidden under a grey cloth cover. The British wore rough khaki serge with long puttees and a flat-topped peaked cap. Many of them favoured a heavy Old Bill moustache.

Now, from their rough trenches along the canal bank, from the houses, from the slopes of the slag-heaps, they opened the aimed rapid rifle fire which was the old Army's pride. The Germans came on as bravely as ever, but the rifle fire scythed into the solid blocks of them and the blocks vanished. At that range the bullets' trajectory was flat, and in that formation each bullet went through two or three men before spending its force. Grey corpses piled up along the canal bank and in the grubby fields. The mist lifted and the sun shone. The church bells kept tolling and the devout, dumbfounded people of Condé and Jemappe, of Boussu and Ville Pommeroeul and Mons kept going to Mass. The Germans reformed and came on. Second and third waves formed behind the first, and came on. The artillery fire grew hotter, louder.

Our men were glad to be fighting instead of marching. This was a Regular Army, yes, but more than half of the men had been recalled from the reserve only three weeks earlier. Civvy Street had softened them, but they had not lost the professionals' steady gait, the back slightly bowed to take the weight of the pack and prevent its straps cutting into the shoulders, knees slightly bent so that the leg never locks and the boot slides along the road instead of pounding into it, lessening heel shock.

And some were not men, but boys, like Drummer Boy Pusey of the Royal

Fusiliers, who had only been allowed to go with his battalion after special pleading to the C.O.; and who now found himself drumming his way across the historic battlefield of Malplaquet and, a little later, across the town square of Mons, marching proudly towards an early wound and a long imprisonment. (After the war he served on, completing thirty-two years' regular service, finishing as a captain.)

Yesterday most of these men had marched 17 miles, and the day before, 21. In the Mons position they had had to dig trenches where they could, and run about the slag-heaps looking for fire positions, often to find that they were too hot to stand on.

For a long time "A" Company of the Royal West Kents held an isolated outpost position against three battalions of Brandenburg Grenadiers supported by artillery. At last the Brandenburgers swarmed over them and reached the canal. Now it was the turn of the King's Own Scottish Borderers, supported by machine-gunners of the King's Own Yorkshire Light Infantry . . . Hotter and hotter grew the fight as more Germans reached the British line, shook out into some sort of attack formation, and came on. The pressure grew all along the 21-mile front, but most heavily in the Mons salient where the canal curved north and east round the town. Here stood the 4th Middlesex and the 2nd Royal Irish.

Mons was not a good place to fight. It just happened to be the spot at which the B.E.F. found itself when it met the German Army advancing in the opposite direction and in much greater strength. The Commander-in-Chief, Field-Marshal Sir John French, had the choice of standing or running. He chose to stand. It so happened that the whole weight of the enemy fell on one of his two corps, and within that corps mainly on the right division, the 3rd; and within that again, on the two battalions in the Mons salient.

Late in the afternoon it became clear that the Germans were too strong to be held up any longer. The B.E.F. would have to retreat. By then the Middlesex had lost over 400 men and the Royal Irish over 300. So, the Army withdrew from its positions. The Retreat from Mons had begun.

This long retreat had its origins in the blind miscalculations of the French General Staff and it was to end, thirteen days later, in the loss of nerve of the German General Staff. Britain's Army, a mere five divisions among the 125 by then already engaged on the Western Front, was as yet too small to mould the form of history, though it could and did add a curve or a line here and there. The basic form was settled by German and French plans for the war, which both had seen coming for many years.

The Germans planned to make a gigantic swing into France, their left "holding onto" Switzerland as a man might swing round a banister, the right swinging in a great arc, first west, then south through Belgium and to the far side of Paris.

The French – thinking that their defeat in 1870 was due to reliance on fortresses, and believing that the soul of France could only express itself in attack – planned to attack, more or less everywhere.

War began. The two plans were put into operation. The French soon came to grief. Nothing that their airmen, cavalry, or spies reported would convince the General Staff that the Germans were doing something different from what had been expected. Their own attacks failed horribly. Only too often they were launched in formations as foolish as the German mass, but without the thorough German cohesion and preparation. The casualties were appalling. During the single month of August France lost over 200,000 men, and, worse, she lost her confidence. The great attack, which was to cut through the Germans like butter, had failed. Instead, the Germans were coming on, disciplined, tough, in endless field-grey hordes.

At this moment the B.E.F. stepped into the line on the left of the French, at Mons. August 23 was a good day in the ranks, and along the battle line. The British soldier had fought a good fight and he knew it. He was not at all down-hearted. But this day were born the distrust and dislike which marred all future relations between the French and British High Commands and even, to a lesser extent, within the British headquarters. It is not hard to pick on scapegoats. Sir John French was a very touchy little man, seeing offence where none was intended. The French general on his right, Lanrezac, was a pessimist who had no use for "amateur" soldiers, by which he meant all foreigners. Major-General Henry Wilson, of the British General Staff, was capable of telling the cavalry that they had not seen what they had in fact seen, otherwise their reports might disturb his preconceived ideas.

The truth is that the Germans were imposing their will on the Allies, and no one knew how to stop them. Meanwhile there was the grim necessity of retreat, day after burning day through one of the hottest Augusts Europe has ever known, on roads choked with long lines of refugees, their belongings in push-carts, babies in arms, women dying of exhaustion in the hedges, dust clogging the parched throats, smoke from burning towns sullen along the northern and eastern horizons and, insistent on the inner ear, the tramp tramp tramp of jackboots, coming irresistibly on.

August 24 – 15 miles. *An infantry division occupied 15 miles of road space. It had 18,000 men and 5,600 horses. A cavalry division occupied $11\frac{1}{2}$ miles and had 9,269 men and 9,815 horses.*

August 25 – 15 miles. This day, while the 18th Hussars were in action dismounted, one of the held horses to the rear broke away from its holder and grabbed a nearby sheaf of corn. Bombardier Taylor of "L" Battery R.H.A., in action nearby, saw the whole stook collapse, revealing some very discomfited German soldiers. Mr Taylor, long since retired, says enigmatically, "They did not get away with it."

Some of the cavalry carried lances and some swords. Many British officers favoured a monocle, though blessed with perfect sight; also a small toothbrush moustache. In the Guards, cavalry, and crack line regiments it was rare to find an officer without at least five hundred pounds a year of private means. Since a 2nd Lieutenant's pay was nine shillings a day, on which he had to dress and live like a lord (which he often was), the extra money was a necessity, not a luxury.

The Forest of Mormal lay in the path of the retreat. The B.E.F. had to split to get past it, Haig's I Corps going to the east of it and Smith-Dorrien's II Corps to the west.

The fog of war, already thick, became dense. (The Official History lists eleven references to "Fog of War". There are only two references to "Flying Corps, R.F.C." – the one organization which, if properly used, could have found out what really was happening. As the American expression has it – it figures.) In the night of August 25/26 the advancing Germans, as ignorant of our movements as we were of theirs, blundered into both Corps' positions. The fight against I Corps was the inconclusive skirmish of Landrecies. The other battle, that against II Corps, was deliberately forced by General Smith-Dorrien.

About three in the morning General Allenby, the cavalry commander, told him that the Germans were close, and in large numbers. Unless II Corps could get away in the dark, they'd have to fight. But the men were dead beat. Many units hadn't yet even reached their appointed positions for the night. Heavy rain added to the exhaustion and the confusion. The retreat could only continue at the cost of losing all cohesion, and by sacrificing the 4th Division. This last had just arrived, to be thrown into the torrent of events without heavy guns, transport, engineers, or a host of other necessary adjuncts.

Smith-Dorrien decided to give the Germans a bloody nose, so that in future they would come on much more cautiously when they knew they were faced by British troops. The right of his line rested on the village of Le Cateau, which gave its name to the ensuing battle.

The night passed in the utmost chaos. A corps of French cavalry spent the whole night crossing the front from right to left. The British formations, some of which were still picking up lost detachments and reforming after the confusion of Mons, kept running into their own transport. The headlong advance to Mons, suddenly turned into a retreat and now as suddenly halted, produced an effect

The British Regular: above, a private (anon.); right, a general (Gen. Sir Horace Smith-Dorrien, commanding II Corps)

like closing the gates of a race course in the face of the arriving crowd and telling everyone to go back the way they came. Worse, II Corps's right flank was floating unprotected on air. Haig himself was in Landrecies with his headquarters when the Germans broke in there. He was not in good condition to stand the strain, since he was suffering from the unromantic but devastating effects of acute diarrhoea. He made his escape from Landrecies believing that its garrison was doomed, and that any delay would see the rest of his corps swallowed up, too. On August 26, therefore, when I Corps should have been supporting the right of II Corps, it continued to retreat, and not even on the same line as before, but farther east – that is, farther from II Corps. The Commander-in-Chief exercised no unifying control.

At Le Cateau the dawn light showed a heavy mist, as there had been three days earlier among the slag-heaps of Mons. But today, August 26, the 568th anniversary of Crécy, gave promise of even greater heat. The regiments stood again in line – the Cornwall Light Infantry, who had withstood the siege of Lucknow; the King's Own Yorkshire Light Infantry, who every August 1 wore the proud roses of Minden in their head-dress . . . Wiltshires, Suffolks, South Lancashires, Lincolnshires . . .

The Germans came on, head down. If von Kluck had had any sound information on which to base his plan, no skill or courage could have saved the four British divisions (three infantry and one cavalry) from destruction by the ten German divisions (seven infantry and three cavalry) which were present in the immediate vicinity. But he didn't, and partly for that reason the details of the battle are extraordinarily opaque. There was little communication, even for those days. In the 4th Division messages had to be carried by the few officers' chargers available. Royal Flying Corps's aircraft spent valuable time looking for generals to whom they could present messages from other generals. When they found the man they were looking for, they landed in the field next to his headquarters, delivered the message by hand . . . and then tried to take off again. Everyone was practically asleep on his feet.

The broad outlines of the battle are clear enough. The 5th Division, on the right, found its flank in the air. From an early hour it came under attack by Germans in Le Cateau and others working round its right rear. The Suffolks, holding the angle of the position in front of Le Cateau, were attacked by machine-guns and artillery from both flanks; and they had had no time to dig deep. On the extreme left the Germans made a murderous surprise attack with massed machine-guns and artillery upon the King's Own. The battalion lost 400 men in a few minutes. Only those who have been privileged to have this great Lancashire regiment under command in battle – as I have – will understand why it did not fall to pieces after such a catastrophe. But it held together and fought for the rest of the campaign, even the rest of this shattering day, with unruffled distinction.

In another sector the fighting was so close that wheel-driver Nobby Clark of 37 Howitzer Battery R.F.A., knowing that there was only one rifle to be shared among the three drivers of each gun, opined, "We ought to be trained to flick the enemy's eyes out with our whips" . . . "And then throw our leg irons at them," a lead-driver added. And all this is as vivid as though it happened yesterday in the mind of Londoner Syd Spraggon, then a driver of the same battery.

After the early shocks, II Corps settled down and for some hours held its line without much trouble. But the unequal fight could not go on for ever. Early in the afternoon the sheer weight of the Germans began to tell. Now came the real problem. How were the troops, locked in close battle with a vastly superior enemy, to break contact and continue the retreat in an orderly manner?

20

It was done by the courage and stubborn skill of the soldiers; by the caution which Mons and the morning's fight had already taught the Germans; and by the unintentional sacrifice of the most exposed battalions. On the right, the Suffolks, attempting to retire, could not make it and were overwhelmed where they stood, fighting to the end. Next to them, the King's Own Yorkshire Light Infantry did not receive the order to retire, so they held their positions. The Germans spent a long time, and many field-grey bodies lay humped in the root-crops in front of them, before the tide could sweep on and over. By then the rest of the division was free and clear.

In the centre it was the Gay Gordons, with some men of the Royal Scots, who did not get the orders. Their division, the 3rd, made its getaway while the High-landers and their Lowland comrades fought for six more hours, until midnight. Then at last they withdrew – what was left of them. By then they were in the middle of the German Army.

On the extreme left that same French cavalry, which had clogged the roads during the night, now extricated our 4th Division by turning round and putting in a smart counter-attack against the onrushing Germans. Here, too, confusion and missing orders played their part. The Warwicks, for instance, did not begin to retire until near 11 p.m. One of their young officers spent three days between the German cavalry screen and their main armies, before escaping to fight again another day, and another place. His name was Bernard Law Montgomery.

Far into the night the German artillery shelled the empty positions along the Le Cateau–Cambrai road. Far into the night II Corps continued its retreat . . . 15 miles before a rest; and this after the battle, and the previous day and night of marching . . . 23 miles the next day; 20 the next . . .

(During one of these marches Bombardier Gare, now living in Wembley, remembers the following sad message about the divisional commander being passed down the line: *Ten minutes halt – General Snow's collarbone broken*. The halt part was correct; the rest of the message should have been, *General Snow's column-of-march broken*.)

At Le Cateau General Smith-Dorrien's II Corps suffered nearly 8,000 casualties, but it gave the enemy the bash on the nose that Smith-Dorrien intended. The Germans never pushed so hard afterwards; and slowly the spring was compressing for the great counter-stroke. Slowly the accumulation of error was swinging towards the enemy. On September 6 the retreat ended. The men of Mons and Le Cateau turned about and started in the opposite direction. The war of the regulars was over. The Great War proper began, in all its illimitable frustration, sacrifice and horror.

THE CASE OF
THE BEARDED CENSOR

It is not often that one is touched personally *by the war in comparatively small matters. But there is one way we are affected by it which is exceedingly annoying. It is when one receives a letter like this!* (Here an envelope marked OPENED BY CENSOR is pasted into Mrs Bilbrough's diary.) *To have strange prying curious eyes reading one's own letters (that concern no one else) is exasperating ! ! !*

A certain Mr J. C. Silber wouldn't have agreed about Mrs Bilbrough's letters concerning no one else. He was a German spy, and his job was assistant *British* military censor, first in London and then in Liverpool. As a young man in South Africa, knowing Afrikaans and English, he got a job as censor and interpreter in the Boer internment camps. Later he was sent to India with 15,000 Boer prisoners, and there picked up a thorough inside knowledge of the British military system, a talking acquaintance with such places as Simla and Dehra Dun, and several written recommendations as a reliable, loyal and efficient censor. Which, as regards the Boers, he was. He had a great admiration for England.

In fact, he was a German from Silesia and when the war started he knew he must do his bit for the Fatherland. He was then in the U.S.A., and at once set out for England, via Canada, claiming to be a French Canadian. On arrival he went straight to the War Office, applied for a post in military censorship and, on October 12, 1914, obtained it. His pass number was 216.

Apart from deliberately dropping cigarette ends on a few blueprints being sent to America he doesn't seem to have done much harm to the war effort. As he plaintively says, again and again, his information was usually misunderstood, ignored, or reached Germany too late to be of use. His attempts to warn fellow spies that the Secret Service was on their trails usually fell on deaf ears. His most ingenious stunt was to photograph documents and send the prints to his contacts abroad, undeveloped but encased in a lined mourning envelope. The recipient knew that the envelope must be opened in a dark room and the mourning card processed; but if a Secret Service man or supervising censor opened it, unknowing, then the information vanished.

Mr Silber wore a goatee, took walking holidays in Derbyshire, and performed

Mrs Bilbrough (by courtesy of
Mrs E. M. Bilbrough)

his duties to the entire satisfaction of his superiors throughout the war. All in all,
he was a nice little man, and I am sure he felt bad about having to read Mrs Bilbrough's letters. In less difficult times she would no doubt have been happy to
invite him to tea.

*England could be tough, too. This spy
was not invited to tea* (by courtesy of
Ullstein)

THE world which thrilled to the news of Mons and Marne was a world in which Europe was first, the rest nowhere. The Americans were quite rich, certainly, but they didn't have any fleet or army to speak of, and spent their energies in mere trade; while the rest of the globe belonged to someone in Europe, either politically or economically.

Europe *was* the world, a world fixed, settled, for ever moulded. There has never been such magnificent certainty, such assured splendour, as were enjoyed by the opulent and the high-placed of the Edwardian era. Especially in England, there was very little bad feeling between the classes, and no sense of revolution round the corner. "God bless the squire and his relations, and keep us in our proper stations" is a bitter jest now. In 1914 it was a sentiment with which most people fundamentally agreed. It was the foundation of society, the rock on which one built one's life and shaped one's outlook. It involved duties as well as privileges, mutual support as well as mutual dependence. It was unfair sometimes, yes, but do away with it, and what would come in its place? Why, chaos! The pushings of the *nouveaux riches,* who might have money but would never know how to give away the prizes at the village fête! Going to the local and finding the cowman jostling the farmer in the private bar when he'd always gone to the public before, and been happy to! Having a chap above you one day and below you next day, like in America where only money counted, so you'd never know where you stood! Your station might not be as good as you'd like always, but if you started pushing into someone else's, what was to stop another fellow barging you out of yours? No, no! God bless the squire . . .

In the cities there were no squires and the working man did not know that England ever had been, or ever could be, a green and pleasant land. All he knew was what he lived and worked in – industrial blight. Yet there was a patriotism fully as intense as the countryman's, and an even stronger race pride and scorn of foreigners. After all, Brummagem and Lancashire and Clydeside made the best in the world and everyone admitted it. The farmers couldn't say that! The poverty, the slums, though appalling, were accepted because they seemed to most to be inevitable. The world was like that and the job was to make the most of it, not go round crying over what couldn't be mended.

What was true of Britain was broadly true of the rest of Europe, modified by the different circumstances. In England, for instance, the Black Death had done away with serfdom five centuries earlier; but in most of Europe only the French Revolution or the upheavals of 1848 had achieved it, and in some backward parts it still existed, there were still landowners with the right of the first night and powers of life and death over their serfs. Nor had European aristocracy ever achieved the flexibility of the British model. British lords were arrogant enough, in all conscience – and powerful, and hidebound, and isolated from the lower classes; but the European aristocrats were far worse in all these respects.

Nevertheless, the ordinary European of 1914 had as much faith in the system as the ordinary Englishman had, and for the same reason. There was as much tradition and as much patriotism, and certainly as much belief that one's own country lay under the special care and favour of Almighty God.

But the German attack on France had already started a process which would in time destroy everything that Europe was and stood for. The process might have ended sooner, before destruction was total, if there had been less deep a fund of faith, of confidence, of trust, to draw on. The men of 1914 really *believed* in much that we (who know how the Great War fed on these beliefs) can no longer accept. And if you really believe, you don't give in easily. You go on . . . and on . . . and on . . .

By the end of 1914 this reservoir of faith had hardly been touched, though all the major combatants had learned an ugly lesson, and suffered a severe body blow. Russia, heavily defeated at Tannenberg, had learned that weight of numbers alone merely meant weight of prisoners to be lost, weight of corpses to cover the battlefield. Germany's heavy guns had smashed the "impregnable" defences of Namur and Liège; but the General Staff, the military brains of the brainiest nation on earth, had failed to achieve the quick knockout blow which the pre-war planning had shown to be essential. The French, full of fire and burning for revenge, had learned that passion availed not against weight of metal handled with skill and backed by courage. They had also learned that their famous 75-mm field gun, of which they had large numbers, was too light to have much influence in trench warfare.

And England, resting secure – not to say smug – behind the guns of the mightiest Navy the world had ever known, received a fierce blow just where it hurt her pride the most . . .

French guns: this is the famous French 75
(by courtesy of the Musée de la Grande Guerre)

British guns

Austrian guns

British people

(by courtesy of Radio Times Hulton
Picture Library)

CORONEL AND THE FALKLAND ISLANDS

"The Southern Ocean's a terrible place," Mr Hawkins said, "always cold, usually snowing or hailing, the wind blowing. And the sea, you've never seen anything like it. Waves as big as mountains! But we were all young then, and it didn't matter."

Mr Hawkins was past 70 when he spoke to me, but as alert and sharp of mind as in those days, fifty years before, when he was Able Seaman Hawkins of the Royal Navy, serving in H.M. cruiser *Glasgow*. The machines at the Royal London Society for the Blind, where Mr Hawkins was time-keeper, made a steady background hum and clatter. We might have been 'tween decks in *Glasgow*.

"I do know what it's like, as a matter of fact," I said, "I've been round the Horn."

"Ah," he said. "It wasn't always bad, though. Juan Fernandez, now!"

Talking, our minds flew back over those 6,000 miles, those fifty years. We talked of an island . . .

The island lies in tropical waters. Its hills, clothed in dense vegetation, plunges steeply into the sea, and on downward into the blue-black depths of the Pacific. It is hot and calm, and large sea birds doze on the rocks. There was a time when only one man walked the short beach; for this island that we are looking at in the

burnished bowl of an old sailor's memory is Juan Fernandez, also called Mas a Tierra, also Robinson Crusoe's Island.

The three-funnelled ship of war *Dresden*, at anchor close under the cliffs, shows the stress of heavy weather and hard service in her peeling paint, battered steel work, jury rig where cables and wires have parted. The ensign of the Kaiser's Imperial German Navy flies from the foremast. It is March 14, 1915 . . .

At 8 a.m. that day, soon after the sun rose, the British cruiser *Kent* rounded the island from the east, the sun behind her. At the same moment the cruiser *Glasgow* and the armed liner *Orama* came round the west side of the cliffs. The ships glided inward, silent. A hoist of flags fluttered up from *Glasgow*'s signal bridge. At 8.5 a.m., having closed to 8,400 yards, *Glasgow* opened fire.

The helpless *Dresden* promptly ran up the white flag; but parleying gained time for her crew to prepare to scuttle her and abandon ship. Then the forward magazine blew up and she started to go down, very slowly. The British ships closed in among the rafts and debris and swirling wreckage.

There was a pig there, Mr Hawkins remembers, a pig, swimming in the sea. It was the Germans' rations, and you hear people saying pigs can't swim but cor, you ought to have seen that pig. Sam Gough from Reading jumped into the sea and got a rope round the pig's belly. We were all lining the side by then. The lieutenant let the lads turn out a derrick and we hoisted Sam Gough and the pig aboard.

"You ate him, then?"

Heavens, no! He was the ship's mascot the rest of that commission. Then I think the skipper took him home with him.

I went from the Royal London Society for the Blind to the Admiralty and spoke with the professional head of the Royal Navy, Admiral Sir David Luce, G.C.B., D.S.O. and bar, O.B.E. The admiral is the son of the man who was *Glasgow*'s captain on that long-ago commission.

The admiral said, "I remember the Dresden Pig well – that was what he was always called. He was an enormous beast and very bad-tempered. He used to go for me whenever he saw me. I suppose I was 10 or 11."

What were *Glasgow* and *Dresden* doing at Mas a Tierra that March day? How did it come about that fate selected them to write the epilogue to the greatest naval drama of the war?

In 1914, as on a hundred other occasions, Britain's naval problems were two: how to live by the sea, and how to move across the sea. To solve them she had the largest war fleet and the largest merchant navy in the world at that time. Germany had a battle fleet in home waters, a few armed liners whose job was to disrupt British shipping, and two overseas squadrons. The most powerful and efficient of these was the East Asiatic Squadron, based on Tsingtau, in China.

Its admiral, Graf von Spee, commanded the armoured cruisers *Scharnhorst* and *Gneisenau,* and the fast light cruisers *Nürnberg* and *Emden.* In 1914 the cruiser *Leipzig* was also in the Pacific, and *Dresden* soon fled thither out of the Atlantic. Escaped from Tsingtau and loose in the trackless Pacific, von Spee detached *Emden* to act as a lone wolf, and gathered the other German vessels to him. His squadron, then, consisted of *Scharnhorst, Gneisenau, Leipzig, Nürnberg* and *Dresden.*

Qn the British side the immense Grand Fleet, based on Scapa Flow, bottled up the main German battle fleet. For the rest, the Admiralty set about the needle-in-a-haystack task of finding and destroying the enemy's lone raiders and detached squadrons.

At first, matters did not go well. Two powerful German warships escaped to Constantinople through the entire Mediterranean Fleet, and helped swing Turkey into the war on Germany's side. *Emden* raided all over the Indian Ocean with great dash, skill and chivalry, sinking many merchant ships but always saving their crews. Other enemy cruisers terrorized the West Indies.

Part of the trouble was that hundreds of British warships were on escort duty to expeditionary forces, which could well have waited while the warships hunted down von Spee. Then, the Admiralty was at odds within itself. Towards the end of October 1914, a disgraceful campaign of slander forced the resignation of the First Sea Lord, Admiral Prince Louis of Battenberg, because of his German birth. Prince Louis, grandson of Queen Victoria and father of the present Earl Mountbatten, was universally acknowledged to be the Navy's finest officer and, of course, a passionate British patriot. To replace him Winston Churchill, the First Lord, brought back into harness the foul-mouthed, back-biting genius, Lord Jackie Fisher. Churchill and Fisher, the two most dynamic characters ever to be fitted into a Whitehall conference room, sat down to study the problems now facing them. How, first, were their steel pawns, the Navy's warships, disposed on the board? One of the ships they surveyed was *Glasgow* . . .

She was built in 1911 and displaced 4,800 tons. She had two 6-in. and ten 4-in. guns, but no armour to speak of. Her captain was John Luce.

"I didn't see much of my father in those days, naturally," Admiral Luce told me. "After he came back, though, he used to take me sailing. He was keen on shooting, too. I remember him telling me that once, somewhere in southern Argentina, he'd gone ashore with one or two others and shot enough geese to feed the whole ship's company."

H.M.S. Glasgow

S.M.S. Scharnhorst

The finest skipper that ever walked a deck, John Luce was, Mr Hawkins said, *and over six feet tall . . . I joined* Glasgow *in Rio in February '14. After we made two or three cruises we headed for home. I was disappointed, thinking I'd hardly got out abroad before I was coming back again. Then we turned back and we heard about the war beginning. The captain spoke to us all. He told us about the ships over in China, the* Scharnhorst *and* Gneisenau *and that lot. He told us how the Germans didn't have any other place to go except across the Pacific. We were bound to meet them, he said.*

Glasgow was alone on the South American station at that time – one light cruiser to watch 6,000 miles of coast. As soon as the war began she headed for the Abrolhos Rocks, a desolate group of islands off the coast of Brazil, used by the Navy as a secret meeting place and coaling station. There *Monmouth*, a heavy cruiser, joined her, and they began a long search for *Dresden*, which, as we know, had in fact slipped past and into the Pacific. And now the armed liner *Otranto* joined in; and now Rear-Admiral Sir Christopher Cradock came down with his flagship *Good Hope*.

Kit Cradock was a bachelor with a torpedo beard and a twinkling eye. He was imaginative, full of wit and energy, the apple of Jackie Fisher's eye, the friend and trusted junior of Jellicoe and Beatty.

All through September, while Cradock's ships hunted *Dresden* up and down the Atlantic coasts of South America, von Spee came on across the Pacific, making feints and misleading moves wherever he might be sighted, so that the Admiralty was protecting convoys against him off South Africa while he was nearing the coast of Chile, 10,000 miles to the east. But, as the possibility increased that Cradock would be the man to meet him, they sent down to him the old, slow battleship *Canopus*.

September 28 . . . At Punta Arenas, the world's southernmost town, Cradock heard that the Germans were using Orange Bay as a base. He sailed, with his whole squadron, at midnight, without lights. The way lies south through narrow channels and twisting corridors, glacier lined. Harsh winds blow down these funnel-like passages and suddenly, round a sharp bend, the waves surge in direct from the Southern Ocean. Snowstorms blind the lookouts, the surface of the sea disappears under hissing sheets of spray, driven by the wullie-wa, fog drops like a white wall, with no warning. The last survey had been made in 1820.

The squadron reached Orange Bay on time. *Glasgow's* log is laconic. *Proceeded towards Orange Bay. 300 revs. 5.0 a.m., hands to action stations.*

But there was nothing there, only the ring of mountains, the whales, and the bitter wind.

Back to the Falkland Islands, to coal. Coaling took the best part of a day, every ten days or so, if the ship was on the move. They shut all the doors and ports and covered all the hatches except the coaling hatches. Everyone, from the 1st Lieutenant downwards, except the men on watch, put on their oldest, dirtiest clothes. Men filled the bags by hand on the colliers. Then derricks hoisted the bags on to the warship's deck, and men carried them by hand to the hatches. All day coal rumbled down into the bunkers, all day the ship swayed and rocked in the roadstead. It took a week to get the coal dust out of the nooks and crannies, and out of the pores of the skin. Then it was time to coal again.

Back to the Horn . . . terrible weather. *Wednesday, October 7, 1 a.m. Lost overboard by accident, Hoses canvas No. 3–5; Branch pipes copper – 3. Wind – SW 8. Sea, 7.* The waves broke off steel stanchions, 6 in. in diameter, as though they were matchsticks. Water got into *Glasgow*'s flour store and for weeks the crew had oatmeal cakes instead of bread.

On, plunging and wallowing, looking now into the Chilean west-coast harbours for the enemy – Valparaiso, Puerto Montt, Coronel. They knew he must be near now. On, all through October . . .

At 1 a.m., on October 31, being at sea off Coronel, *Glasgow* picked up *Leipzig*'s radio call sign, very close. She reported to Cradock, who was not far off with *Good Hope, Monmouth* and *Otranto*; but *Canopus* was 400 miles back, repairing her old engines. The admiral ordered *Glasgow* into Coronel, to pick up messages from the British consul and hand in others for despatch to London.

At 6.20 p.m. *Glasgow* entered Coronel. A German merchant ship flashed the news of her arrival to von Spee. All five German ships, which were close indeed, hurried to cut her off. They arrived too late, for on November 1 *Glasgow* rejoined Cradock 50 miles out to sea.

So, at last, the stage for the battle was set. Von Spee thought he had only *Glasgow* to deal with, and Cradock thought he had only *Leipzig*.

The squadrons sighted each other at 4 p.m. on November 1. The wind blew strong from the south-east and a heavy sea was running. Cradock could have turned and fled, falling back on *Canopus*, his battleship. According to many, he should have, for he was badly outgunned. But that was not Kit Cradock's way, nor the Royal Navy's. Cradock must also have calculated that even a little damage inflicted on the Germans so far from any base would have crippled them.

He may have been right. But there was to be no damage, not even a little.

For a few minutes the British had the sun behind them and the German gunlayers were looking into its red, blinding orb. But von Spee held off until the sun had set. Then, at 7 p.m., *Scharnhorst* opened fire. Her third salvo wrecked *Good Hope*'s forward turret. *Gneisenau* struck as savagely at *Monmouth*. The British ships plunged on in silhouette against the afterglow while the Germans blurred into the eastern dark; and these ships had won the German fleet's gunnery prize. At 7.50 an explosion on *Good Hope* sent flames and debris 200 ft. into the air. Soon after, she went down with Kit Cradock and all hands, her colours flying. At 9.28 p.m. *Monmouth* went down with all hands, her colours flying. *Otranto* and *Glasgow* escaped to the westward. They were entirely justified in their flight, as, with the heavy cruisers gone, they would both have been sunk before they could even get within range. But the men aboard them were bitter, angry, and from that moment dedicated to revenge. Von Spee had suffered not one casualty, not even a man scratched.

The curtain comes down on Act I.

Von Spee, sailing next day to be fêted and feasted by the exultant German colony in Valparaiso, was offered a toast to the damnation of the British fleet. He said instead, "I drink to the memory of a gallant and honourable foe." And a strange lethargy began to overtake him. He had humiliated the Royal Navy, Britain's pride. He had but to move fast to spread more disaster and humiliation on the other side of the Horn. The British wireless stations, coaling bases and. merchant shipping lay bare to him. *Canopus* and the cruisers could only run away or be sunk. There was nothing closer than Gibraltar or New York capable of stopping him. But he hung around in the Pacific, and every day his fate took on more definite, more ominous shape.

Everything went wrong for the Admiralty that week. The battleship *Audacious* was lost on a mine: German battle-cruisers bombarded Yarmouth: *Emden* sank a Russian cruiser actually inside Penang Roads – and now this off Coronel – a palpable defeat.

Goaded and grim, Churchill and Fisher sprang to action. A flood of orders poured out from the Admiralty. One of these orders, outweighing all the others in importance, snatched from the Grand Fleet, and sent southward with all speed, two ships which could both catch and sink any of von Spee's – the battle-cruisers *Invincible* and *Inflexible*. With them went a new commander, Vice-Admiral Sir Doveton Sturdee.

The avenging fleet gathered at the Abrolhos Rocks. *Carnarvon* was there, wearing Rear-Admiral Stoddart's flag. *Cornwall* was there – *Kent, Bristol, Defence* . . . *Glasgow* rejoined, after repairing her battle damage in Rio. On November 28 the fleet headed south, the battle-cruisers keeping wireless silence so that their presence would not be suspected. On December 7 they reached the Falkland Islands. *Canopus* was already there, berthed on the mud as a fixed fortress, with lookouts on the cliffs and marines ashore to repel land attack.

By now, at last, von Spee had rounded the Horn and was heading north,

Coaling

The Dresden *pig*
(by courtesy of Mr Hawkins)

planning to attack the Falkland Islands. At last . . . and in spite of all his delays, hardly twelve hours too late; but too late nevertheless, finally and disastrously too late.

At 8.30 a.m. on December 8 the lookout on the leading ship, *Gneisenau*, sighted the wireless station and a cloud of coal smoke. At 9 a.m. he saw tripod masts.

Tripod masts meant battle-cruisers. At that instant, the sea being calm, the time early in the morning, and the season mid-summer, von Spee's fleet was doomed. The battle-cruisers were faster, and their guns were heavier, with longer range. A Nelson might have seen that the only hope was to go straight in and fight inside the harbour, with the certainty that enough damage would be done to prevent any serious pursuit of the German survivors – if there were any. But von Spee turned and ran.

The British ships sailed as soon as they could clear from the colliers alongside and get steam up. A stern chase began. At 12.47 *Invincible* and *Inflexible*, having come within range, opened fire on the slowest German ship, *Leipzig*. With great gallantry von Spee turned his heavy cruisers to fight, ordering the light cruisers to scatter. *Invincible* and *Inflexible* settled down to destroy *Scharnhorst* and *Gneisenau*. The heavy black smoke drifted across the sea. A full-rigged sailing ship, like a white ghost from the past, passed between the bellowing steel monsters. At 4.17 p.m. *Scharnhorst* went down and at 6, *Gneisenau*, both with colours flying. There were 200 survivors out of about 1500. The British lost one man killed and two wounded.

Sturdee's cruisers, meanwhile, had split up in pursuit of their German opposite numbers. *Bristol* went after, and sank, two supply ships. *Glasgow* and *Cornwall* took on *Leipzig* and after a long hard chase, and intricate, skilled manoeuvring to avoid damage while inflicting it on the enemy, sank her at 8.35 p.m. *Dresden*, the fastest ship of the Germans, fled so fast that none of the British ships could catch her, so none made the attempt. *Carnarvon* stayed with the battle-cruisers.

That left *Nürnberg* ship-to-ship against *Kent*. *Kent* was considerably the bigger and more powerful of the two, but *Nürnberg* was supposed to be a knot faster. The first battle had therefore to be won in the engine room.

Mr Terrell lived quietly in a flat near the "Elephant and Castle" when I visited him, but that day he was a stoker in *Kent*. *We burned the furniture in the ward-room*, he said. *We burned the companions – ladders – and had to put canvas covers over the hatches else men in a hurry would have put their foot on to a step that wasn't there. We burned everything wooden in the ship, to make the fires hotter. After a long time I felt the guns firing and I knew we'd won. I sneaked up on deck to take a look. Our funnels – we had three tall ones like the* Monmouth *that went down at Coronel, she was our sister ship – were white hot and sparks were blowing back down wind. Someone had left a great jar of brandy on deck there. I took it to the sick bay and were they pleased to see it! Then I went back to the stokehold. I saw holes clear through the ship. I went on shovelling coal and trimming coal from the far bunkers to the engine room bunkers. I worked twelve hours in the stokehold that day.*

Stoker Terrell and the rest of *Kent*'s black gang had wrung 5,000 more than the maximum rated horse-power out of her engines, so that she had reached 2 knots above her designed speed.

So the day-long chase ended. Raked and racked by the heavier British guns, *Nürnberg* lowered her colours and, at 7.27 p.m. sank. Captain Allen could not lower his boats until the shot and shell holes which riddled them had been repaired. Only seven Germans survived. The *Kent* had four killed and twelve wounded, and Stoker Terrell and his mates had had all the hair burned off their legs. It never grew back again.

In drifting rain squalls, with wind and sea rising, the British ships headed back for the Falkland Islands. One German ship remained of that proud and magnificently led squadron which had harried the eastern seas and inflicted the first defeat for over a century on Nelson's Navy. That lone ship, *Dresden*, had an appointment at Mas a Tierra. Night fell.

Survivors from Gneisenau *in the water: this picture, taken from* Invincible, *shows* Inflexible *in the background*

LADY WITHOUT HATRED

1915: *It seems to me that everyone who happens to be alive in such stirring epoch making times ought to write* something *of what is going on! . . . Terrible as it all is, I think I'd rather be living now than say in early Victorian days! Now everyone* is *living and no mistake about it; there's no more playing at things. "Life is real and life is earnest," and I doubt if it will ever seem quite the same again . . .*

1915: *One cannot be thankful enough that one has no relatives fighting at the front. How* awful *that would be! How one would cry out against the injustice of fighting. I would cry out against even patriotism itself. Patriotism is a very fine thing in the abstract, but is it –* can *it ever be stronger than love?*

The most beautiful words about patriotism and love are engraved below a statue outside St Martin's in the Fields. The woman of the statue has good eyes, wide set and level, rather a long nose, a wide jaw; not a beauty – too strong a face for that – but good-looking, with tremendous character, and, if touched in the right place, with duty done and time to relax, then there would be humour.

Her name, of course, was Edith Louisa Cavell. She was 48 when war broke out, and had for years been living in Brussels as Directrice of the Red Cross hospital and head of a school for nurses. She soon became involved with a group of noble Belgians who were smuggling refugees out of their German-occupied country, first the British stragglers from Mons and Le Cateau, then young French and Belgians who wished to join the armies. There is no doubt that Nurse Cavell allowed her hospital to be used as a "station", where these men were hidden for a night or two before being passed on out to Holland. Half a dozen different villains are supposed to have betrayed her; and all probably did, but the whole operation was so quixotically and openly carried out that the Germans must have known about it almost from the beginning.

On August 15, 1915, they arrested Miss Cavell and held her prisoner, incommunicado. From here on it is a story of the German authorities, headed by von Bissing and von der Lanckem, doing all in their power to ensure that a veil of secrecy should hide Miss Cavell until they could tear the veil aside and reveal, not her person but her corpse. On the other side the U.S. ambassador, Brand Whitlock, his assistant Hugh Gibson, and the Spanish ambassador, the Marquis de Villalobar, fought like men possessed to save her.

The Germans held the trial in secret. The judges' names were kept secret. The attorney appointed to defend Miss Cavell mysteriously resigned "owing to unforeseen circumstances". His successor was not permitted to see her before the trial, nor to inspect any of the documents in the case, nor to know what she was accused of!

To all inquiries, von Bissing and von der Lanckem knew nothing . . . they were out . . . they were busy. But in the evening of October 11, while they were telling the Americans that sentence had not yet been passed, in fact it had – Death, to be carried out that same night. Whitlock was seriously ill. While Gibson and Villalobar fought with high words and scornful rage for Miss Cavell's life, nearly coming to a fist fight within the Germans' mansion, the Rev. H. S. T. Gahan entered Miss Cavell's cell and gave her Holy Communion. They sang together "Abide with me". She wrote her last letter, one of mankind's proud witnesses – "I have no fear nor shrinking; I have seen death so often that it is not strange or fearful to me . . . But this I would say, standing as I do in view of God and eternity, I realize that patriotism is not enough. I must have no hatred or bitterness towards anyone."

At 5 a.m. the Germans took her from prison to the rifle ranges 2 miles outside the city, and, after making her observe the execution of a fellow conspirator, shot her. The mighty and obtuse Teutonic nation had killed a nurse, and roused a world.

MARCH 5, 1916: *Conscription in England has come! One can hardly realize it, things have come so gradually. Voluntary recruiting did well, but not well enough, and the slackers* had *to be got at somehow so thanks to Lord Derby's scheme, all those who wouldn't enlist will be* made *to. But the Government have felt their way to this great step very cautiously, very guardedly, and have made absurd concessions relating to men bearing arms who may have "conscientious objections" to war!*

Mrs Bilbrough's fine scorn for the Conchie is very typical of the time, and so is her use of the word "slackers". While only too much aware of its horror, people were still able to think of the war as a sort of game, and put the selfish or scrupulous or fearful on a par with the half-back who wasn't tackling as hard as he might, the cover-point who wasn't putting enough zip into his return pegs to the wicket keeper. In a word, there was enthusiasm.

We are taking a look at the years 1915 and part of 1916. The great step of conscription didn't come until the end of this period and by then it was too late. Britain had already lost, in the dumb anonymity of private soldiers' uniforms, hundreds of thousands who should have been officers and trainers, thinkers and planners and leaders. Appallingly wasteful and unfair though it was, simple undirected enthusiasm was enough to get the men into the armies and the armies into the trenches and, when necessary, out of them and over the top – until 1916.

There was stalemate on the Western Front, but as yet no despair. It was a time of improvization rather than invention. Some new-fangled weapons came into use, but they were mainly handled by old-fangled thinkers. Objects grown familiar in the roles of peace (buses and drifters and kings) were drawn into war service, for the war had begun to take over, to infiltrate every corner of life. Really, only the war existed. Everything and everybody was a part of it: it included everything and everybody. Men fought and marched in Africa, Asia, the Pacific. Men dug defences for London, and that really brought it home to one, didn't it? Men died in old ways and in new.

During the period a great deal seemed to happen – in Rumania, Gallipoli, Mesopotamia, for instance, but at the end not much really had. The Allies still faced the Central Powers across a smudged, dirty gash that marred the earth from Switzerland to the sea. Soldiers still died and caught lice and got trench feet, and generals still racked their brains to think of a way to achieve a victorious campaign . . . or if not a campaign, a battle . . . well, an advance . . . a successful patrol encounter . . . something, anything.

In only one place did the war flourish – the air. There a new science, a new art, a new breed, flowered together in red flame and blue sky . . .

British Marines at Ostend, August 1914

British troops attack, Gallipoli
(by courtesy of Ullstein)

*German naval airship flying over
warships*

Hull of airship, with Lewis gun ready
for action

Bodies of civilians murdered in Serbia
(from Covenants With Death)

Constructing defences round London

Ford convoy on the Jebel Hamrin, Mesopotamia

The German East African campaign:
King's African Rifles

Turkish front: a helio in use

*Camel Corps with Indian Lancers,
Sinai Desert*

London buses used to transport troops
near Ypres

British Armed Trawlers at Dover

Victor Emmanuel of Italy

The Kaiser with the Sultan

Ferdinand of Bulgaria (*in Austrian
uniform*) with Charles of Austria (*in
Bulgarian uniform*)

The Tsar

Nicholas of Montenegro

Ludwig III of Bavaria

The wounded arrive at Charing Cross

WAR
IN
THE
AIR

Here's a letter written home to his parents by a young artillery lieutenant, John Baker, then attached to the Royal Flying Corps:

Sunday 29 October, 1917 . . . I've had a most thrilling day. I went up for the first time here, and did a 3 hours patrol over the trenches. Coming back the landing signals were out wrong and we proceeded to land down wind . . . We proceeded to shoot down the aerodrome at about sixty miles an hour. Our engine had cut out so we could not take off again, and we shot over a ten-foot bank at the bottom of the aerodrome. The machine went clean head over heels. I landed about 10 yards away on the back of my neck . . . I saw Lewis hanging by his belt upside down in the machine, his head and shoulders buried in the mud, and petrol and oil pouring over him. I simply lay back and roared with laughter . . . I could imagine him wondering where he was and trying to swear through the mud. However, I undid his belt and we were neither of us hurt in the least except that I cut my chin a little . . . I have resumed a blade of the propeller, which was of course smashed, and I am going to have a walking-stick and photo frames made out of it. You can tell I'm all right by the fact that I played "soccer" for the squadron after lunch.

Here's another, written on April 18, 1918:

I was given a whole day off yesterday. About two o'clock in the afternoon they tried to wake me up, but as I knew I needn't, I simply could not, and so I slept the clock round until I had to get up for the early patrol this morning. . . . I don't think anyone could get so tired as I've been in this last week. I'd rather fight the guns for 18 hours a day than fly for 6 under the conditions we have had to during the Huns' late excitement. But, though half of us are "somewhere else", the other half is just as cheery . . . I hope you haven't been anxious at all. There's never any need to be 'cos bad news travels much quicker than good, doesn't it? Nearly all my old pals have gone.

Hardly six months separate those two letters; yet they contain a capsule description of the first air war in history; of the men, the machines and the tasks; of the emotional content, which stretched from the starriest wild-blue-yonder thrill to the dead-weariest mechanical performance of a job grown hateful; of nerves strung like screaming piano wires (yet, to the very end, still the blue sky known to be there, and attainable, beyond exhaustion and fear); of youth; of a boundless three-dimensional future . . .

The four years of the Great War saw the development of military flying from the cradle to a powerful maturity. In 1914 they flew things like elaborate kites. The pilot sat in the open air, in full view, on a sort of bench. The kite had a motor-cycle engine tied to it. Most pilots flew unarmed, though some aggressive characters carried a pistol or cavalry carbine. Meeting an enemy machine in 1915 Lieutenant Sholto Douglas could raise his hand in salute, fly on, and think nothing of it. The German did the same. What else was there to do? When machine-guns were eventually mounted in aircraft, they could not be fired through the propeller. The observer therefore sat in front, firing the gun backwards and upwards over the pilot's head. Later, the pilot was put in front and the machine-gun was mounted to fire forward but at an angle, to miss the propeller. The pilot could not fly directly at his target, but at an unknown and incalculable angle to it. Guns frequently jammed and, until a non-freeze oil was produced, could not be fired at all in cold weather or at high altitudes.

The frustration of these conditions, exploding in the tensions of aerial combat, caused some wonderful reactions. Pilots tried to, and did, ram each other. They fired pistols and hurled grenades. Being unable to harm his German enemy any other way Lieutenant Baker once flung a full Lewis gun drum at him. It would certainly have done the German a mischief if it had hit, but it didn't; it nearly took off Baker's own tail plane instead. And a pilot of 60 Squadron, travelling from an old aerodrome to a new one with some valuable camp equipment – a piece of Nissen-hut chimney – stowed away in his craft, found a use even for that, when all else failed. He pointed the length of pipe at the enemy and fired his Very pistol down it. It must have looked as though the British were now carrying howitzers in their aeroplanes. The German fled.

Flying speeds were of the order of 60 m.p.h., landing speeds about 30.

All this changed at an ever increasing rate through the war years. By the armistice the Royal Air Force possessed a four-engined bomber, the Handley Page V/1400, capable of flying from Norfolk to Berlin and back, with a bomb load

Bleriot XI-2 Series 2

Farman S.7 Longhorn

considerably heavier than an entire 1914 machine. It possessed fighters with a performance in the region of 150 m.p.h., and carrying multiple machine-guns. It possessed, too, a philosophy of war and a type of flyer who were to come together, for the saving of the nation, in 1940.

In 1914 military flying was based simply on the fact that being up in the air flyers could see farther than men on the ground. Thus, their first job was to find the enemy troops and contact our own. In the early days of Mons and Le Cateau, as we have seen, the generals were equally ignorant about both. The airmen were also used to carry urgent messages, or those which could not be delivered by other means. This responsibility, of observing and reporting, occupied the bulk of the Royal Flying Corps throughout the war. The work was done by Corps squadrons, as they were called (because they were allotted on the basis of one to each Army Corps), containing three flights of six machines each. The organization was flexible, but in principle two of the flights were used for artillery observation and one for trench observation.

This was the daily chore of about three-quarters of our airmen . . . to go up in a two-seater of very ordinary performance, fly the 20 miles or so to the front, then spend hours cruising backwards and forwards, ranging our guns on enemy batteries, reporting such things as the movements of enemy infantry and the locations of newly built pill-boxes. Mostly it was boring. (Here is young Baker, to his mother, on November 8, 1917: *I'm jolly certain no one will be gladder than me to get away from this beastly district. I have just landed from a 3½-hours flight, and you can't imagine how boring a limitless expanse of shell holes and water can look, when you gaze at them for 3½ hours.*)

Sometimes it was anything but boring: when Archie fire suddenly rocked the fragile craft; when a fine spray of petrol showed that a lucky ground machine-gunner had hit the tank; when the red-nosed killers of Richthofen's Circus dived out of the watery sun at the sitting ducks of the Corps squadrons. And there was another, more bizarre peril. So thick was the concentration of artillery on the Western Front that the air became dense with their shells, German and British, on their way to ground targets, and at a certain height aircraft were in very real danger of being struck by them. Every pilot of that era has recorded the extra-ordinary sensations – of hearing the shells incessantly pass, rumbling like Tube trains; of seeing them in the air, the big ones like boilers on the loose; of feeling the bump as they went by; and, grimly, of seeing a friend's craft disintegrate, struck by one.

Then there was aerial photography, a new gimmick found invaluable by the Army on the ground. At first the pilots used to cut a hole in the floor of the machine for the camera; later it was mounted on the side of the fuselage. The

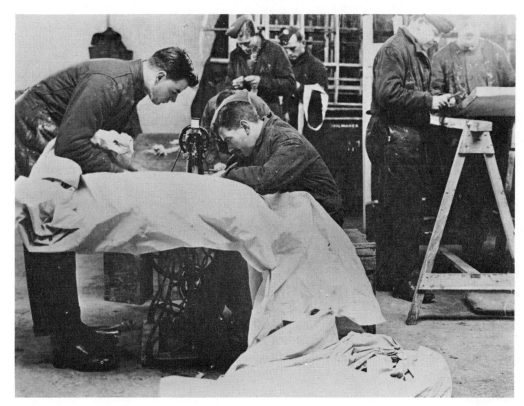

*Air mechanic/sailmakers cutting out
fabric for covering planes*

Plane overturned in a gale

pilot changed plates by reaching out, pulling a lever, and pushing it forward again. Lieutenant Sanders describes it: *The aeroplane is travelling but slowly against a strong head wind . . . The reduced speed on the outward journey is of great assistance to the pilot in getting his exposures accurate, and when he turns westward again, having reached the farthest point that he wishes to photograph, his machine is whirled back to our side of the trenches before the enemy gunners can correct their aim.*

(But this was an exceptional day. Normally the wind blew from the west, wafting our machines towards the lines and Germany, but hindering their return.)

The flyers strafed front-line trenches and rearward supply columns. They dropped bombs by day and, increasingly, by night. They did whatever an imaginative staff, barely convinced that men really could at last fly, asked them to. (Baker, in March 1918: *Had to go up on a comic stunt this morning. I had to fly low over the German trenches to attract the fire of their machine-gunners. As soon as they opened on me, our gunners turned on to them and blew them up . . .*)

Gradually it became clear that these "comic stunts" and "priceless flips" depended for their success on a measure of dominance in the sky. Hence were born the long-range bomber and the true fighter, then called the Scout. The bombers never really reached strategic depth – though they were poised to do so, with the big Handley Page, when the war ended. The Scouts formed the habits, and the spirit, that won the Battle of Britain.

Trenchard, the R.F.C. chief in France, insisted that Scouts should not be used as close escort to bombers or Corps planes. That was a defensive mentality. They were to carry the fight to the enemy, attacking deep over the lines, destroying enemy Scouts wherever they found them. This policy left our Corps planes unprotected, and accounted for the very high scores of the German aces, above all of Richthofen – who could sit back, wait for the British to come to them, and then choose as their prey the weak, the new boy, the straggler, the lost and strayed, while refusing battle with the strong, and those in good formation or an advantageous tactical position; but it gave the Royal Flying Corps the mastery of the air. Here is how they used it (this is Lieutenant Mayberry of 56 Squadron describing his actions on July 31, 1917, the first day of the battle of Pilckem Ridge):

. . . Crossed the lines over Ypres at 500 feet just underneath very thick clouds. Got into the smoke from the artillery barrage and found it impossible to see ahead at all. . . . Dived down to about 30 feet and flew straight along the road to Gheluwe . . . Two E.A. (enemy aircraft) *Scouts appeared from over Courtrai and attacked me. . . . From Bisseghem I went north-east and immediately saw Henle aerodrome . . . Circling round the aerodrome the only sign of activity I could see was one man lighting two smoke fires. This man looked at me but did not seem to take any particular*

*The impression left by an airman
falling from a Zeppelin*

61

Rittmeister von Richthofen

notice. I came back along the line of the southernmost sheds and dropped my first bomb . .

After this, Mayberry's exploits make one dizzy. He attacks the airfield up and down, back and forth, endways and sideways. He attacks two staff officers on horses, naturally causing the horses to bolt. He falls upon a company of infantry, twice, as it marches along the road. He attacks an aircraft on the ground. He has a brisk dog-fight with another enemy Scout, shoots it down, then attacks the crowd of Germans who collect round the wreckage. He shoots up a passenger train. And then home for more ammunition, more 20-lb. bombs and, probably, three or four more little excursions.

All this in a sky that the airmen turned into a surrealist dream with the bright colours of the new warfare. British aircraft's wheels were often painted red, white and blue, the spinners blue. The Germans seemed to be imitating butter-

Captain Albert Ball, v.c.

flies, with red bodies, spotted wings, and squares of black and white or black and yellow on the tails. Some were mauve all over, some had green and brown patches. Others, like Richthofen's plane, were bright red.

This was the sky of the first true air-fights, made familiar to two generations by such films as *Hell's Angels* and a dozen like it. The face, the costume, the action, is as familiar to us as a matador's in the bull ring. There is the whirling disc of the propeller, behind it the flying-helmet, the lady's silk stocking streaming from it. The goggles peer flatly over the muzzles of two machine-guns. The guns stutter in vicious fire. Below the goggles the ace's thin lips part in a sardonic smile. He raises one gauntleted hand in farewell to a gallant, doomed foe . . .

It really was like that, too. This is Captain Molesworth of 60 Squadron . . . *Our leader got into his favourite position, and the rear Hun hadn't the ghost of a chance. The next instant he was a flaming mass. We simply had it all over the Boche*

Von Richthofen's funeral . . .

". . . an awful doom . . ."

for speed and, as we had the height, they could not possibly get away. I picked my man out as he was coming towards me, and dived straight at him, opening fire with both guns at close range. He suffered the same fate as his companion.

A burning machine is a glorious but terrible sight to see – a tiny red stream of flame trickles from the petrol tank, then long tongues of blazing petrol lick the sides of the fuselage, and, finally, a sheet of white fire envelops the whole machine, and it glides steeply towards the ground in a zigzag course, leaving a long trail of black smoke behind it, until it eventually breaks up . . . Somehow, you do not realize that you are sending a man to an awful doom, but rather your thoughts are all turned on that hateful machine which you are destroying, so fascinating to look at and yet so deadly in its attack.

They didn't have any parachutes, either. But the speeds were so slow that there was always some hope, even after a machine took fire in the air. Lieutenant Gower won the V.C. and very nearly saved his pilot's life in just such a catastrophe. Their machine, piloted by Sergeant Mottershead, caught fire at 9,000 ft. over the trenches, the flames at once setting light to Mottershead's clothes. Gower stood up in his place and sprayed Mottershead with the fire extinguisher all the way down to the ground. Here Lady Luck finally turned her back. The forced landing threw Gower clear but pinned Mottershead under the now fiercely-burning machine. Still Gower tried to save the pilot, crawling towards the flames and working the fire extinguisher over Mottershead; but there was too much flame. Mottershead died.

The aerodromes were cow pastures. A run of about 400 yds. was needed, and of course there was only grass for surface, though ashes and cinders were spread in the worst of the Flanders autumns. Everyone lived in Nissen huts. The machines stayed out in the open, or in canvas hangars like overgrown tents. Inside the tents, when it was wet or foggy, the canvas covering the wings and fuselage, usually taut as a drum, hung flabby on the frame members, glistening with pearls of condensation. Metal fittings were dull and tarnished, waterproof covers encased each separate blade of the wooden propeller, and tarpaulins draped the engine.

The fitters worked on the engine, the riggers on the "craft", tightening turn-buckles, stretching canvas, loosening wires, shaping wood. All wore dirty brown overalls, as did the few armourers and that man of marvels, the wireless mechanic. (The Corps planes had a wireless transmitting set by which the pilot Morsed back to the guns; but the guns could only communicate with him by setting out strips on the ground, in a prearranged code.)

There was as yet no idea of standardization in aircraft, and the cow pastures grazed a wonderful menagerie of aerial beasts. In April 1917, for instance, the

R.F.C. were flying five marks of the old B.E.2; also the D.H. 2 and 4; the F.E. 2d and 8; the excellent and beautiful S.E.5; Spad; Martinsyde Scout; Sopwith 2-seater, Pup, and Triplane; Nieuport 2-seater and Scout; R.E.8 (this was the usual Corps machine); Morane Parasol, which was glumly described as having the gliding angle of a brick; and an early mark of another great craft, the Bristol Fighter.

None of them was reliable, by modern standards. Here is an excerpt from Lieutenant Sanders's log-book for September 25, 1916, flying from Droglandt Aerodrome:

4.5 p.m.	Machine No. 4428	20 mins.	Shoot – Dud engine
5.15 p.m.	„ 2755	25 mins.	Shoot – Dud engine
6.20 p.m.	„ 2755	15 mins.	Engine test; air mechanic as passenger.

Another day Sanders was forced back twice, the first time by "dud" weather, the second by a "dud" machine. The third time out he completed the mission – but the craft overturned on landing. Another entry laconically records, *Engine failed. Hit a haystack.* The more senior Major Sholto Douglas (but still only 23) went one better than that: he hit a horse. John Baker has a note for February 6, 1918 – *we had four crashes today, but nobody hurt.*

The windshields had no wipers, of course. When it rained or snowed the pilot leaned out to look along the side. The early models of the Constantinesco interrupting gear, which enabled machine-guns to fire through the propeller arc, were not very reliable, so pilots frequently shot holes through the propeller, instead. In the frantic dives and twists of air combat speeds were reached far in excess of what the materials then in use could withstand, and the flyers frequently saw a comrade's wings come off, and machines disintegrating in air. The wind, as I have already mentioned, was always in their minds. After all, when your speed is 90, a 45-m.p.h. head-wind halves it. The prevailing westerlies, combined with Trenchard's implacable orders to carry the fight to the enemy, resulted in the loss of many a British machine, and the saving of many a German.

The aircrews wore an astonishing variety of uniforms. The majority favoured that of the regiment from which they had been seconded to the R.F.C., though most probably owned and sometimes wore the Corps's own distinctive double-breasted "maternity jacket". For flying they wore over the uniform a leather coat, a close-fitting helmet of leather or canvas, goggles and fleece-lined boots. Clothing regulations were not regarded as the Word of the Lord. The C.O. of 60 Squadron once went up on dawn patrol, unshaven, wearing pyjamas, a bur-berry, bedroom slippers and snow-boots. When he landed a general's cere-monial inspection was in progress. There was an unpleasantness. Otherwise, I feel, the C.O. would not have bothered to mention his dress as anything out of the usual.

The Scout squadrons had the big names – Ball, McCudden, Bishop and Mannock. These were the new Galahads, the darlings of the nation. The publicity was not of their seeking, but in the spectacular nature of their calling it could not be avoided, and it also served to focus and strengthen the national morale. It became embarrassing for Corps and bomber pilots, though, when a girl-friend asked one of them how many Huns *he* had shot down. He could only shuffle his feet and mumble unhappily. How could he explain that he wasn't equipped to do more than defend himself, and that not well? How could he make her understand what it was like to watch the ground, listen to the engine, fly the machine, work the wireless key, change the photographic plates, hear the rumble of passing shells – while at the same time, all the time, the observer scanned the sky, ready to call for a dive to shelter our own side of the lines at the first sign of an enemy Scout?

They were young, very young. Most had reached France at the age of 18 or 19. Sanders's log-book shows that he had twenty hours of dual and five hours of solo when he was sent to France as an operational pilot. (In Hitler's War it was rare for a pilot to go on ops. with less than 500 hours.) Death was always near, but it only put a greater pressure on their youthfulness. Sanders and his observer used to pelt each other in the air with pellets of silver paper, each trying to make the other think it was a stray bullet or shell splinter that had caused the sudden sting. They were men; but they fought and argued over bars of chocolate. Everyone used a wonderful jargon, which became the basis for English slang throughout the 1920's . . . *The C.O. is horribly bucked with our efforts, old man. Jolly good set of pictures . . . went west . . . put up a stout show . . . let's organize a bust . . . Well, old bean, I had my first trip with my flight commander over the lines. My word! It was "some" trip, too . . . put the vertical gust up the old Hun . . . dud . . .*

They threw "bloody wonderful drunks" and bedded down with mademoiselles, madames and the farmer's daughter. But there weren't all that many females available, and their high spirits were natural far more than they were alcoholic. Here is 60 Squadron celebrating the award of the V.C. to their ace, Billy Bishop . . . *After dinner we had a torchlight procession to the various squadrons stationed on the aerodrome. This was led by our Very light experts . . . We charged into one mess and proceeded to throw everyone and everything we came across out of the window. We then went over to the other squadron. The wretched lads were all in bed, but we soon had them out, and bombarded their mess with Very lights, the great stunt being to shoot one in through one window and out at the other. After annoying these people for a bit, we retired to our own mess, where we danced and sang till the early hours of the morning. I have still got a piece of plaid cloth about 6 inches square, which was the only thing left of a perfectly good pair of "trouse" that belonged to one of our Scotch compatriots . . .*

They wrote letters which must have caused their mothers to weep. Thus John Baker, finding himself alone in mess with a friend and no staff. . . . *We cooked our own meal; poached eggs on toast. The water we poached 'em in wasn't quite hot enough, but they weren't bad; then fried Bully Beef mixed with toasted cheese which was awfully good . . . inadvertently put the milk saucepan back when we had made the coffee, and it boiled over . . .*

But, when all is said and done, these men are remembered, and their service is a glorious one, because they did their duty. Many died. Some survived, to become great men in the councils of the State. The rash, touching, gallant youngsters of the old log-books and faded letters are now Marshal of the Royal Air Force Lord Douglas of Kirtleside, Air Chief Marshals Sir Arthur Sanders and Sir John Baker; men who, under the strong hand of "Boom" Trenchard, moulded the Royal Air Force.

The R.A.F. came into existence on April 1, 1918, with the amalgamation of the Royal Flying Corps and the Royal Naval Air Service. It was born in the stress of the last and mightiest German offensive on the Western Front, the first land battle in which the air arm played a truly decisive part. The offensive began on March 21, 1918, and the R.A.F. was soon thrown in. (Baker, March 26: *We suddenly had orders to send every available machine to bomb and machine-gun a few thousand Huns who were massing to attack. The sky was simply filled with our machines. I think we must have put the vertical gust up the Germans all right – 200 aeroplanes suddenly appearing and opening up on him.*

Aerodromes had to be abandoned in a hurry. The Germans concentrated their best squadrons in support of the offensive. New R.A.F. pilots, straight out from England, flew forward at treetop height, ignorant of the ground and the fast changing positions, to be shot down in droves by German machine-gunners on the ground and Fokkers waiting above.

John Baker's poignant letters tell what happened; and, between the lines, why we won . . . *You can't think how we long for a rest now. I can't get the blinking hum of the old machine out of my ears any time . . . I don't know why my brain gets awfully useless in the evenings now after flying, sort of headachy . . . Poor old Money's mother has written to me to ask if I will send home his little dog . . . There are about 18 little dogs running about the camp and I don't know a bit which particular one he favoured. Also, I've no idea how one sends a little dog home from the B.E.F. . . . We are mixed right up in it and my brain simply won't write things. I do nothing but fly and sleep with rare intervals for food . . . Don't worry any, my*

*Home people. We are going to get the old Hun cold, though it will cost us a bit . . .
One of our observers got a D.S.O. for flying the machine back and landing it
perfectly, when he himself was very badly wounded, and his pilot sitting in front of
him with his head blown off . . . I was up at 6 o'clock and have been at it pretty
straight until now – 5 o'clock. Even now some of our machines are getting ready for
night bombing.*

Baker won an M.C. during that great battle, and the R.A.F. won its name and
fame. The Great War lasted several months more; and afterwards there came
another war; and again let the young man who was to become an Air Chief
Marshal speak for the spirit of the R.A.F., in 1918 as it was in 1940 . . . *It's a
great game, and I'm gladder than ever that I can carry on at this time.*

An R.E.8 setting out on night flight

CAMEL BITES PILOT

Well, there was no doubt there was a raid in progress and a pretty big one too. Overhead there was a swarm of aeroplanes looking like a flight of bees – or butter-flies. But the noise! I shall never forget it . . . Gracious heavens, what next! A wild fight in the air thousands of feet above the earth! – in things like fearful distorted mechanical birds (only with no beauty) which were circling round each other and engaged in deadly combat; dodging, swerving, diving, and roaring, while sometimes they would be lost sight of in a cloud of smoke.

Thus Mrs Bilbrough, writing on July 7, 1917. If she felt like that in England, you can imagine what the effect was in the Sudan. There the Air Age met the Stone Age on May 23, 1916, and fought it to a kind of draw. A small British expeditionary force was in the process of chastising a rebellious Emir called Ali Dinar. The Army advanced in the classic square across the desert, and had covered 120 miles in this fashion, into the very heart of the enemy country. But for the last two days the supporting aircraft had not been able to find the Army in the dust and haze. Today it was 2nd Lieutenant Slessor's turn to try.

The B.E.2c biplane's wheels left the ground punctually at 5 a.m. and in that instant mankind's newfound mistress, the air, opened her arms to the 18-year-old at the controls. The dust fell back, and the sullen heat of the African desert, and the endless thorn scrub, and sand and flies and sores and starvation. The young man was entering at the same moment upon this magic, incumbent air, upon his manhood, upon war . . . The myriad stars gave depth and pattern to the domed sky. Steel moonlight rimmed the engine cowling. Red light from the exhausts tinged his face and glowed in his goggles. The cylinders throbbed and the tappets danced in line down the engine in front of him.

Dawn broke. Slessor throttled back to cruising revs., sighed, and set about his business. Near 7 a.m. he saw flashes in the haze below, and knew that it could only be the Army's screw-guns in action. Then, with sudden clarity, he saw a plain covered with men on fine horses and riding camels. Their black and grey and white robes streamed out behind them as they galloped away from the gun flashes. They saw Slessor, too, and fired upwards at him, holding the long rifles with one hand and the reins in the other. Slessor dropped bombs and fired his Lewis gun.

A B.E.2c taking off on the North West
Frontier

And there was the city, Ali Dinar's capital . . . and there, beyond, a seething mass of Dervishes . . . and the giant banners of Ali Dinar . . . and the man himself, on his great white camel! Slessor dipped the biplane's nose, let go his last two bombs, and pressed the trigger of his Lewis gun.

The bombs burst under Ali Dinar's camel, blowing it to bits, though Ali Dinar himself was miraculously unhurt. The Dervish Army suddenly became a frenzied, panic-gripped mob. They were already defeated; now they were routed, and that was the end of the campaign.

At that instant an enemy bullet, fired from the ground, passed through a pile of mail on the floor of the aircraft and pierced Slessor's right thigh. Blood poured out, soaking the mail. Slessor flew the plane in spasms, meantime extracting and tying on his first field-dressing. Soon he found that he could not use his right leg to press the rudder bar for a right turn. He couldn't use his left leg to pull that end of the bar towards him, which would have had the same effect, because he had had polio as a child, and the leg was never much use.

He found he could control the machine by reaching out and grabbing the wires that led from the rudder bar to the rudder pylon. It was very turbulent and he got airsick. The flow of blood dried up after a time, but he was pretty tired when he landed, after $5\frac{1}{2}$ hours in the air.

I asked Marshal of the Royal Air Force Sir John Slessor how he got into the Royal Flying Corps with a polio disability. He replied inscrutably, "I had an uncle in the War Office." Asked about the wound he said, "They took the bullet out with a large knife. There was no anaesthetic. A couple of bottles of hot champagne and a swig of brandy had to do instead. The operation was bad enough, but the hangover . . . that was really awful."

JUNE 7, 1916: *The worst news we have had since the war began reached us today, and all England is electrified with the shock – sudden and awful – that Lord Kitchener is drowned. He and his principal staff were on their way to visit Russia, and when off the Orkneys at night, and in a rough sea and gale of wind, some evil German submarine torpedoed and sank the vessel they were on, and none were saved except two of the ship's crew . . .*

Actually there were a few more survivors than that, and it was a mine that sank *Hampshire*. But Mrs Bilbrough was right, as always, in her emotional response. Kitchener of Khartoum's death removed from the scene the last giant, the last man the British public had faith in. When we were looking at the War in the Air we had to go past ourselves, so to speak, to the end of the war; but in fact we are in the middle of 1916, and the character of the war is changing. So is the character of the people everywhere.

Kitchener's death made everyone examine the rest of the war leaders more closely, and to do so was to emphasize what experience was proving: there were no more Kitcheners. In July the battle of the Somme began, lasted four months, cost oceans of blood, and achieved nothing. Earlier, at the end of May, the main fleets of England and Germany at last came to grips in the battle of Jutland. England, expecting another Trafalgar, was bitterly disappointed at the dubious outcome. The German fleet never ventured out to sea again, but that was hardly a Trafalgar. Jellicoe, the Navy apologists reminded everyone, was the only man on either side who could lose the war in an afternoon. In truth, the sheer size of the battle fleets, the sheer mass of steel and volume of money involved, seems to have turned the admirals' thoughts to caution, to that course of safety which in war is almost always the most dangerous to pursue. And, of course, Jellicoe was no Nelson. Britain fought on, no longer morally strengthened and upheld by the belief that her Navy, at least, was undisputed mistress of the seas.

At the Front, a remorseless logic built the stalemate like a dungeon round all thought and existence. After the battle of the Marne in 1914 the generals had tried to continue the war of manoeuvre. The soldiers, striving gallantly to obey, found that it could not be done. Two new weapons of war – machine-guns and barbed-wire – prevented movement. Ah, the generals said, we shall use heavy artillery to blow up the machine-guns and destroy the barbed-wire. It didn't work . . . More guns, then, heavier shells, more of them . . . It didn't work . . .

The nations of Western Europe were highly industrialized and they had a superb network of rail communications. Their factories could turn out as many guns as there was room for at the Front. Their railways could carry forward as many shells as relays of gunners could fire off. They could also transport reserves more quickly to a threatened spot than the attackers, trudging across a belt of country which their own shell fire had made practically impassable, could move forward. The cavalry waited in reserve for the great break-through. It never came.

The generals acted like apes familiar with nails, confronted for the first time with a screw. The problem was very real but the answer attempted was seldom, "let's try something different"; it was rather, "let's try the same thing that didn't work last time, but more so". Whenever something different was given a proper and bold trial, it worked. Whenever the "more" was tried the results, foreseeably, were the same – but more: more destruction, more mud, more corpses, more prisoners, more shattering of minds and bodies.

Through 1916 and 1917 despair steadily grew, and justifiably so. No one was controlling the war. It was controlling them, for its own purposes of unlimited, endless, universal death.

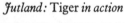

Jutland: Tiger *in action*

Lord Kitchener, as Sirdar　　　　　　　*Admiral Sir John Jellicoe*

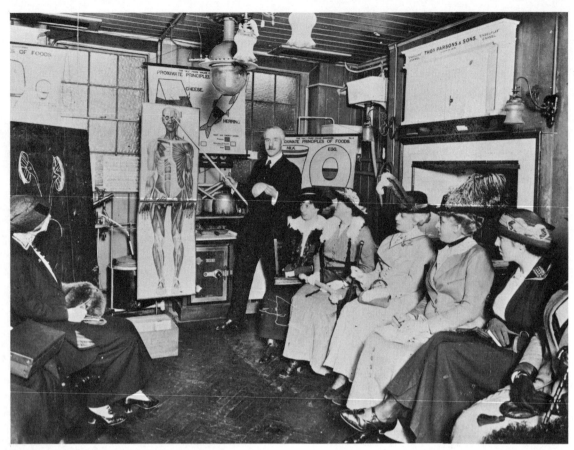

A lecture for Red Cross Nurses

Collecting at Newmarket

Listening for enemy mining
under the trenches
(by courtesy of Ullstein)

77

Machine guns . . .

78

. . . barbed wire . . .

. . . heavy guns . . .

. . . shells . . .

Machine guns . . . barbed wire . . . heavy guns . . . shells

. . . lead to stalemate

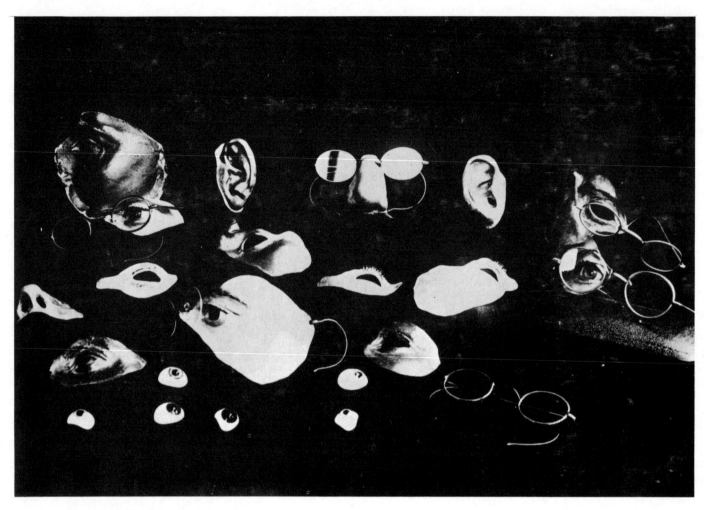

Various plates and attachments for
"renovating facial injuries"

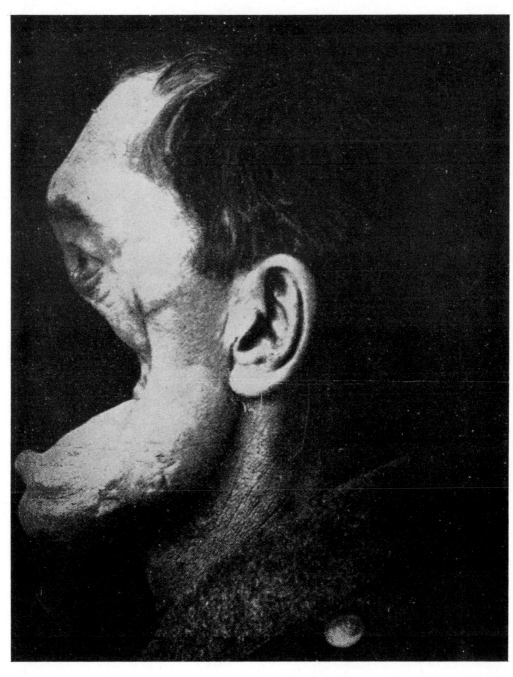

A facial injury (from Nie Wieder Krieg)

PASSCHENDAELE

When I went to look at Polygon Wood, forty-seven years after, the trees had grown quite tall again. I met a gamekeeper walking down the silent aisles, checking his weasel nooses and polecat traps, for the wood is a pheasant farm now.

Outside Passchendaele they were digging up the road to put in drains. A car with GB plates had stopped near a mechanical ditch-digger. The young couple in the car watched the work with fascination but the older man with them seemed to be urging them to drive on. I guessed why. If you dig in that part of Belgium you know what you're going to turn up. For the old man it wouldn't have been just a skull or a bone, it would have been one of his pals, it would have been a terrible memory, it would have been his own youth.

I went to Hill 60. There a local shopkeeper has preserved a few yards of winding trench, its sides falling in, full of corrugated iron and rusty souvenirs. A small fee secures admission and the elderly man in grey flannel trousers, sports-jacket and quiet tie had paid his fee but didn't seem to be getting his money's worth. He was just wandering round, head bent, looking neither to the right nor the left.

"Were you here – then?" I asked him. He nodded.

"What regiment?"

He looked up and his eyes sparked. "60th Rifles," he said. I asked if I could know his name, then, and where he came from. But he relapsed into private communion and shook his head and walked away. He may have gone there to remember, but now that he had remembered, he wanted to forget.

Perhaps it was right that he should remain anonymous, for anonymity, destruction without name or fame, was the rule of the Great War, and particularly of this battle which I was reconstructing, the Third Battle of Ypres, 1917; also known as Passchendaele.

Passchendaele sums up the Great War in itself, because Passchendaele is courage and sacrifice beyond understanding; Passchendaele is the ultimate in acceptance, in discipline; Passchendaele is mud, sleet, lice, mud, noise, jagged steel, horror piled on reeking horror, men and animals torn in pieces, mud seeded with brains and blood, mud heaving with putrefying thousands of fathers, sons and lovers; Passchendaele is appalling muddle, waste to terrify the soul. A German general described it as *... worse than Verdun ... the greatest martyrdom of the World War.*

How did it come about? Why were British troops (British in the widest sense, for a heavy load of the battle was borne by Australians, Canadians and New Zealanders) committed to endless attacks where success was either unlikely, valueless, or both? To answer, we must go back a bit. Back to the stalemate, and the reasons for it . . .

The nations grappled, like half-paralysed lunatics, on the Western Front. It was a world war, but the doctrine of the decisive point had prevented the generals from letting their imaginations leave that sanguinary cockpit. They could think only of the Western Front, and they could think only of the mass attack. To suggest there might be a way round, in another theatre, was almost treason. To suggest that a better method than the mass frontal attack *must* be found was to show loss of nerve. Imagination had come to be regarded not as the ally of courage, but as its opposite.

So, in Flanders fields, courage was being cut down, and with it other trees which would not grow again – the centuries-old, slow-matured trust between classes; a social structure that accepted the good intention even where the deed was unworthy or foolish; a friendly Britain. The privates and the generals of 1917 had alike grown up in a world where to question was to doubt, and to doubt was to undermine this basic strength, which had given Britain growth and some change without revolution. But this war demanded the mind which will not accept, which prods and probes into the very roots of act and motivation, and has no reverence.

In all countries the bloody stalemate drove the political leaders to desperation. Generals were sacked and replaced by others with more mellifluous promises and more imposing jaws. The most specious of all was the French general, Nivelle. Nivelle had the answer, Nivelle said. There would be a Big Push, on the Nivelle Plan. The whole French Army would take part. The Germans would fight for a few moments, then their line would crumble, the cavalry would break through, *la guerre finie.*

On April 16, 1917, the French attacked, like swords of flame. The attacks failed miserably, totally. The flame went out and the sword broke. The French Army mutinied. The new French military chief, Pétain, told Haig the true state of the French Army. Haig kept it from his own government as "a military secret", a matter for soldiers only, and continued to press Lloyd George to accept his plan for a huge offensive in the Ypres salient. This plan had originally been prepared for use in 1916, and it depended on strong French co-operation.

Lloyd George, like a fish on the hook, tried to wriggle away from the ghastly prospects – longer casualty lists, more butting into the steel wall, more angry men dragged away from industry and farm to end in mass graves . . . He considered sacking Haig, but who would replace him? All the other generals, at least those known to the civilian leaders, were cut from the same cloth and would follow the same methods and give the same answers. And, incredible though it may seem, Haig was popular with the men in the ranks. He had determination. He meant to beat the Boches and win the war; so did the troops, who recognized the fellow-feeling. He had utter confidence in the British soldier, and the soldier responded to this dangerous faith – dangerous to the soldier, that is – by trusting Haig's generalship.

In fact Haig had four disastrous faults. He was an incurable optimist. He saw only what he wanted to see. He had a devout sense of mission, and hence an inner conviction that he was always right. And he had no imagination. Seven years after the Great War he was still insisting that the horse would always be important in war – "the well-bred horse," he added, very characteristically. His idea of grand strategy is best summed up in his own words: "We should follow the principle of the gambler who has the heaviest purse, and force our adversary's hand in and make him go on spending until he is a pauper." (It didn't look quite so obvious, or quite so clever, at the front. Listen to Sapper John Hunter of the Royal Engineers: *We lay listening to the bombardment and the tramp tramp of the infantry going past . . . drooped shoulders, eyes bulging, faces unshaven, the snappy step replaced by a stagger . . . They keep tramping into the jaws of death. More crosses are erected. R.I.P. is the epitaph.*)

There is no doubt that in 1917 something drastic had to be done to take German pressure off the French. There is no doubt that the Admiralty would have been very pleased if the Army could have captured the strip of Belgian coast between Nieuwpoort and Zeebrugge, so that the Germans couldn't base U-boats there. Haig's plan – to clear the Belgian coast, attacking from Ypres – would certainly attain both these objects, if it succeeded.

What no one, looking back, can understand is why he hoped to succeed. The year before, on the Somme, the British Army attacked for four months, suffered 400,000 casualties, and advanced an average of about 3 miles on a front 20 miles wide. Nothing had happened, and nothing was proposed, that would alter this state of affairs – but the men were now expected to advance 35 miles, the first 15 of them in under two weeks.

(The medical services were investigating what really constituted lousiness, in an average division after 6 average months of hard work, rest, and action in various parts of the line. 95% of the men examined were infested and the average lousiness was 20 lice per man. 5 of the men in every 100 were found to have on them from 100 to 300 lice each. Clean shirts became reinfested, as badly as before, within 2 days. The average soldier's blanket contained .8 of a louse.)

Lloyd George argued; Haig and the Chief of the Imperial General Staff, Robertson, insisted. At last, with reluctance, Lloyd George agreed to the great offensive – and must therefore bear the final responsibility for it. He did, however, order that Haig must not attack except in conjunction with the French, and that he must stop the offensive if it began to slow down or suffer disproportionately heavy casualties.

These curbs meant nothing, because Haig had risen above Prime Ministers. He *knew* the French Army would not co-operate, and that was not an argument against the offensive but the main reason *for* it. No amount of casualties would deter him, because no casualties could be disproportionate, when the offensive meant the saving of France, and hence the Allies.

The wheels were set turning. Slowly at first, then with increasing speed, the British Army rolled towards its fate, its Commander-in-Chief confident, determined and blind, at the controls. On May 13 he took the main role in the offensive away from the careful, realistic General Plumer, who knew the ground well and had no visions of pie-in-the-sky, and gave it to the thrusting cavalryman, Gough, who had hardly seen the area before. On June 2 Pétain told him that the French Army could not fulfil its promises. On June 7 he began the attack.

On that day nineteen mines, averaging 21 tons of explosive each, were blown up under and behind the German front line on the Messines Ridge, to the right (south) of the Ypres salient. By the end of the day we had advanced an average of 2 miles on a front of 6 miles. It was an auspicious beginning. The Anzacs played a great role, and suffered half the 24,500 casualties incurred. There had been a plan to exploit any success at Messines without delay; but this plan was allowed to lapse. The Germans were given ample time to make thorough preparations on their new line.

(Listen to ex-Private X, of the 63rd Division: *The first ripple was blotted out. The dead and wounded were piled on each other's backs, and the second wave, coming up behind and being compelled to cluster like a flock of sheep, were knocked over in their tracks and lay in heaving mounds . . .*

But on June 12 Haig reported that Germany was almost beaten, her armies hardly more than a disorganized rabble. *This being so,* he said, his attacks must continue, as it was reasonable to expect that one more push would cause the Germans to collapse. Now, it was barely a month since the War Office had submitted to the Cabinet a different and much more accurate estimate of German strength. According to this, one more push would *not* cause their collapse. How was the contradiction to be glossed over, so that Haig could have his way? Why, it was easy! General Robertson advised Haig not to talk about the state of the Germans, but merely to insist that there was no alternative to his plan. The Cabinet could hardly intervene, as yet. They had much else on their minds . . . Italy was not doing well in the Alps, Russia was heading towards revolution, France remained jittery.

The curtain went up again on July 31, to reveal a land rising gently to the Pilckem Ridge dead ahead and the Gheluvelt Plateau on the right. Running across the front were a number of small streams, their names all ending in *-beek*, which means brook. No sort of surprise, such as the mines had achieved at Messines, was planned. Artillery preparation had begun on July 16. 3,091 guns took part, firing four and a half million shells. Haig and his staff were astonished to be told, afterwards, that the bombardment had disturbed the soil and formed craters and, indeed, when it rained, even mud.

Shell hole and shell burst, Polygon Wood

Passchendaele: above, *June 1917;*
below, *December 1917*

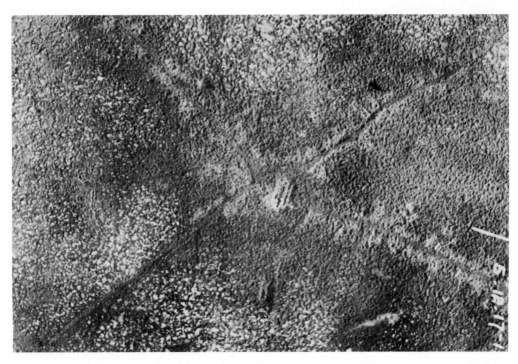

*British cavalry awaiting orders to move
forward*

Polygon Wood, September 1917

The opening of the final barrage made the loudest man-created noise till then heard on earth, rivalling the explosion of Krakatoa. The earth heaved, the skies opened in livid flame. It was 3.50 a.m. A moderate breeze blew from the west, and dense low clouds obscured the sky about 500 ft. up. The infantry climbed from the trench to the firestep, from the firestep to the parapet. The barrage advanced. The whistles blew. Two cavalry divisions stood ready close behind Ypres.

In the afternoon it began to rain. Some objectives were taken, some were not. It rained all August 1 and 2. The British held whatever positions they had reached, often on very unsuitable ground, against heavy counter-attacks.

(Listen to Sapper Hunter, digging trenches: *It looks like a graveyard I told Jock, who told me just to slice the bodies through at each side of the trench and not to bother digging any more out. The odour was awful and the more we dug the more dead men's bodies we had to go through.*)

The casualties were 32,000. (Casualties at El Alamein were 13,560, for a battle that lasted a week.) Captain N. G. Chavasse, v.c., m.c., of the Royal Army Medical Corps won a bar to his V.C. – a posthumous bar. Despite severe wounds, from which he later died, he went out again and again under heavy fire to find and bring back the helpless wounded.

(A survivor speaks: *You've never seen rats till you've seen rats that were born, and fed, and grew in human flesh.*)

Haig described the day as highly satisfactory and the losses slight for so great a victory. His Intelligence chief, Brigadier-General Charteris, wrote in his diary, "All my fears about the weather have been realized. It has killed this attack. Every day's delay tells against us . . . Every brook is swollen and the ground is a quagmire." It was true. Under the shelling and the rain the innocent *beeks* were turning into dangerous bogs. The Gheluvelt Plateau remained in German hands. The attack on it was set for August 10.

On that day the assaulting troops, though attacking with all possible courage, failed to make their objectives. Where they did, the Germans boxed them in with artillery and machine-gun fire. Supplies, ammunition and reinforcements could not come up. The Germans then wiped out the lodgment with a strong counter-attack. Prisoners were few on either side. They had to be escorted back through the enemy's fire. Instead, they were taken round the corner and shot. The escort had a rest and then returned, to report that the prisoner had been killed by shelling. He probably would have been, too.

(Listen to Major Carrington, M.C., of the Royal Warwicks: *Every scrap of news coming down from Passchendaele told of futile struggle with the swamps of the salient, of useless tanks bogged in the slime, of mismanaged partial attacks, of hopeless plans and angry generals, of great losses in men and small gains even in ground.*)

The assault continued. August 16, 17, 18 – Langemarck, near the north end of the salient. Some success, but on August 24 the Germans counter-attacked and retook most of the earlier gains.

Both the Army commanders concerned with the battle, Plumer and Gough, now recommended stopping. Haig repeated the importance of the Gheluvelt Plateau, and gave back to Plumer the task of capturing it. Plumer asked for three weeks to make his plan and preparations. Gough's 5th Army, however, continued to attack all day on August 27, like a punch-drunk fighter who cannot stop pawing at the dimly seen, punishing enemy. The result was more bitterness, more casualties, and no ground gained. It rained steadily. The assaulting infantry had to wait ten hours on their forming-up lines, thigh deep in mud, under shell fire; and this with no objective, no purpose. If, by a miracle, they had succeeded, no one would have known what to do about it. But of course they didn't succeed.

Casualties for August were 26,000, making 82,500 for the offensive so far. In four weeks the advance had averaged about 2 miles all along the 15-mile front. The Prime Minister asked Haig to consider stopping. He asked him to consider sending troops to Italy to help the Italians. Haig insisted on keeping every man and gun he had, and demanding more.

(Listen again to Sapper Hunter: *We went outside and found him* [a lance corporal] *huddled up in an empty dugout. "Come out," Jock called to him. He didn't move, but glared at us like a scared animal, his teeth chattering and hands clinched together, letting out a low moan more like a growl at intervals. This was a usual sight.*)

The assault continued. September 20 – Menin Road Ridge. Objective captured. German counter-attacks all that day and all through September 25 . . . repulsed. The operations, conducted by Plumer, went as well as could be, in the circumstances. Casualties – something over 20,000.

The assault continued. September 26 – Polygon Wood, another bite at the Gheluvelt Plateau. This day the Australians bore the brunt. They took Polygon Wood, beat off the inevitable counter-attacks, and held on. Casualties – 15,375. Advance – about a mile on a narrow front.

Haig was exultant. The German defences in Flanders were near the breaking point, he said. The Germans were suffering. We were wearing them down. (But listen to Lieutenant Fisher of the 42nd Bn. Australian Imperial Forces, talking about some survivors of the Manchesters: *Never have I seen men so broken or demoralized. They were huddled up close behind a box in the last stages of exhaustion and fear . . . the dead and dying lay in piles. The wounded were numerous – unattended and weak, they groaned and moaned all over the place . . . some had been there four days already . . .*)

The assault continued. October 4 – Broodseinde. Success to the extent of another mile deep, 7 miles wide. But no one cared any more. Casualties – 12,000. A squadron of King Edward's Horse were brought up to within 150 yds. of the Steenbeek and waited there for the break-out to open country. Most of the horses were killed and the squadron went back on foot.

The assault continued. October 9 – Poelcapelle. No appreciable gain. The West Riding Division, attacking against uncut barbed-wire and unlocated pill-boxes, lost 2,500 casualties and by early afternoon was back where it had started from.

On October 4 the rain set in for the winter, a steady cold rain with icy winds. By this time the battlefield had absorbed about eighty million shells (twenty million more were to come). Both Army commanders again pressed to end the campaign; but Haig noticed that the enemy were in possession of the Passchendaele ridge. Let them just be cleared off that, and then there would be better winter quarters – high ground, no mud, a good lateral road behind the front. No one seems to have pointed out that assaults on the ridge would certainly create mud where none had been before. No one pretended, either, that there was now any hope of achieving the Belgian coast.

The assault continued. October 12 – Passchendaele. The rain fell harder.

Ground gained – nearly nil. Casualties – 10,973. Hundreds of fit and unwounded men lost their lives by drowning in the mud while going up to the line. And not only men. Mules and horses were drowned. Guns vanished by the battery, swallowed up in the heaving ocean of mud.

The assault continued. October 26 – Passchendaele again. October 30 – Passchendaele . . . Very cold now. High winds blowing. The Canadians going over the top at 5.50 a.m. . . . November 6 – Passchendaele. November 10 . . . the South Wales Borderers suffer ten officer and 374 other rank casualties, a battalion of the Munster Fusiliers thirteen and 400. The Guards Division completes its record of taking every objective it has been given throughout the offensive; it has lost 4,500 casualties doing it. The Canadian Corps has had 12,404 by now.

The desirable winter-quarter ridge remained just that step away, but now, at last, an outside power intervened. The Italians collapsed at Caporetto and troops had to be sent at once to keep Italy in the war. Haig, at last, was forced to stay his hand. On November 20 the offensive in Flanders came to an official end.

Zeebrugge was not now 35 miles from the Ypres front, as it had been in June: it was 30 miles. The British armies had suffered 244,897 casualties to achieve 5 miles; of those, some 75,000, being killed, missing, or shattered in mind or body, were gone for ever. The conditions of the battle, and the battlefield, may be judged when you realize that after every recognizable body and readable identity disc had been given separate burial, the records showed that 35,000 *more* men had vanished without any trace at all. This was on the British side only. The German casualty figures were grossly exaggerated, for the purpose of protecting Haig and his doctrines. In fact they probably suffered about two-thirds of ours.

So, if Haig meant to force the Germans to spend lives, he had done it. If he meant to prevent the Germans attacking the French, that too had been achieved. But if this is generalship, why don't lumbermen fell oak trees by butting them down with their heads?

The British Army stood like spent animals in deep, freezing mud outside the little village of Passchendaele. Haig's policies had destroyed all trust between generals and politicians, all faith between the leaders and the led. In March the following year the Germans nearly swept the disheartened and now distrusting Army aside. Once again only Britain's ultimate weapon, the obstinate courage of her people, saved the nation. When Walt Whitman penned the following lines he was writing about a duel between American and British ships, but his lines apply equally well to the British Army in Flanders: *Our foe was no skulk in his ship I tell you, . . . His was the surly English pluck, and there is no tougher or truer, and never was, and never will be.* It is a proper epitaph, and a summing-up, of the terrible battle of Passchendaele.

Haig

Exhausted soldiers

SWEETHEARTS AND WIVES

Friday, January 19, 1917: Last evening I was sitting alone over the fire, just dozing comfortably after a cold and cheerless day, when without any warning there came the most ghastly crashing explosion possible to imagine! . . . I tore upstairs to look out of one of our upper windows which faces the direction of Woolwich, and sure enough the sky was all red and lurid and vibrating, *and then I felt sure the arsenal was blown up and the whole of Woolwich in flames !!*

Actually it was the Silvertown explosion, and Mrs Bilbrough was about twenty miles from it. It is impossible to imagine what it must have been like inside the factory. Nor is it necessary. Mabel Lethbridge has described just such an explosion in an ammunition factory . . . "a dull flash, a sharp deafening roar and I felt myself being hurled through the air, falling down, down, down into darkness. . . . In the glare I saw girls rise and fall shrieking with terror, their clothing alight, blood pouring from their wounds . . . I made an almighty effort to rise, catching at some machinery with my hands. The sickening stench of burning flesh met my nostrils . . . The machinery I was holding was red hot . . . Burnt, bleeding and tortured, I reached the doors and tried to force them open, but the metals were twisted by the intense heat . . . Swiftly, surely, the flames crept nearer . . . Was something lying across my legs that I could not rise? I tried desperately to free them, tugging at the left one, which appeared buried in a wet mass of blood and earth. It lifted easily in my hands, so easily, so light . . . My leg had been blown off and I held in my tortured hands the dripping thigh and knee . . ."

These ghastly infernos made the headlines, but the real revolution was going on in the accountants' offices and the board rooms. It was a revolution of, by, and for women. The great industrialist Sir William Beardmore said, "The actual output by girls, with the same machines and working under exactly the same conditions, and for an equal number of hours, is quite double that of trained mechanics." The Great War freed women from a thousand age-old taboos, a hundred humiliating restrictions, and the girls of the munition factories and arsenals were in the forefront of that liberation.

It didn't always go easily. Sometimes the men in a plant did all they could to delay the inevitable. The foremen would give the girls wrong or incomplete

Damage from the Silvertown explosion

instructions; none of the men would lend tools or help fix broken-down machines; sometimes the girls were sent to Coventry. (One angry young woman
reported that the men nailed up her drawers and poured oil over everything in
them; but this surely must have been an unusual, if pleasingly bizarre, punish-
ment.)

At the time, many "slackers" undoubtedly feared that if women were proved
capable of doing their work, they would find themselves in the trenches. But this
attitude was the exception. As a rule, the few men left as supervisors and setters-
up did all they could to help, and the girls settled happily and quickly into a new
and wider world.

The revolution was social as well as economic. In the war factories, for the first
time, the girls of Britain's great industrial cities met the daughters of the landed
gentry. The former, the pros who needed the money, were nicknamed Khaki
Girls, the latter Miows. Again, there was friction. Some Khaki Girls thought
that the Miows were there to spy on them, to take away their jobs, or – worst of
all – to improve them. They didn't want or need to be improved. But on the
work-bench, sooner or later, everyone found her own level and showed her true
worth, and was accepted at it.

Upper-class complaints about the "preposterously high wages" of city working
girls ceased as soon as a Miow was on the bench herself. Wages actually varied
from about 15/- a week for beginners on a 6-day 8-hour shift, to about 43/- a
week for a 12-hour night shift. 30/- was probably the average. In the Y.W.C.A.
canteen, sausages and mash was $2\frac{1}{2}$d.; mince and mash – 2d.; beans – 1d. A girl
would be fined 2/6 for leaving her machine before the hooter went, and 2d. for
loitering in the cloakroom. Full board and lodging in a hostel was 14/- to 18/- a
week.

Everywhere the girls made their little islands of individualism and femininity,
affirming themselves as women – in the flowers arranged in shell-cases, in the
ribbon binding their hair, or the flower at the waist, or the edging of lace on a
butcher-blue overall. In a thousand ways, from bigger cloakrooms to more
honest supervision, from cleaner factory floors to better light and heat, they
improved the lot of all factory-workers, men included. And, most important,
they had led the fight in which women were to shake off their chattel status.

Wrens painting mines and shell floats

Women workers
in the "howitzer shop"

Woman grave-digger

Woman blacksmith

104

Women road-workers

*Women workers at
the Royal Arsenal, Woolwich*

106

*Miss Lilian Barker, Lady Superintendent
at Woolwich Arsenal* (by courtesy of Radio
Times Hulton Picture Library)

Woman brewery worker

The first "clippies" (by courtesy of
Radio Times Hulton Picture Library)

Women heaving coal

WAR – *war – war, and our brave lads are being hacked and shot down day by day in appalling numbers. One wonders if there will be any men left at all in the world at the present rate of extermination? It will be a world of women before long –* What an awful place ! !

Mrs B., you are wonderful!

... Already, before Passchendaele, Britain had lost an ally and gained an associate, as revolution took Russia out of the war and increasing involvement brought the United States in. But in neither case was the real impact felt until 1918.

... Despair deepened into numbness. Perhaps it was as well. I doubt if the Western-European participants could have survived the blows and shocks of 1918 unless they were protected by a certain inability to feel, their national nerve ends not so much bruised as ground out of existence.

... It was a time of inventions now, rather than improvisations. Men of science and engineering, or at least men who understood them, came to be given an increasing influence. They had to be, because the old-fashioned type of mind, military and civilian, did not speak the language of radio mechanics, of aerodynamics, of the internal combustion engine. They needed interpreters; but they saw to it that the new men never attained anything like real control.

... One new invention was the human female, the species we habitually refer to as "women"; or rather, women were re-discovered. For about nine centuries they had been hidden behind the poses and postures which the Age of Chivalry had found poetically essential for them. Now chivalry was dead and real women emerged again, and were found to be just what they had been in the Dark Ages, and before: man's other half, stronger in some things, weaker in others, as much concerned with life and death as he, and as capable of making wise decisions about them. We have glanced at women in the factories. The photographs, following, will show a few of the other jobs they did. What the photographs do not show is the all-important change of attitude, both in men and among women themselves.

... The war continued. We have seen how Germany's U-boat campaign provided a sort of excuse, at least in the beginning, for the long agony of Passchendaele. It actually, and genuinely, and justifiably, was the reason for another, brighter action ...

Blockships at Zeebrugge

ZEEBRUGGE

April 23, 1918, which is St George's Day without a doubt, and perhaps Shakespeare's birthday . . .

Many ships came into Dover Harbour that morning, gliding slowly past the cliffs to anchor under the grey castle on the hill. All were warships and many showed traces of recent battle, in twisted steel and blistered paint. But one ship looked more like an abandoned hulk than the light cruiser she actually was. She had no masts, her three riddled funnels leaned at drunken angles. Sheets of discoloured metal flapped in the ship's roll. Her sides were gouged and punctured.

She moved, and appeared, lop-sided, for while her starboard side was comparatively clear her port side looked like the aftermath of a fire in a tenement – hung and festooned with wreckage, bent ladders, dangling wires, shapeless scorched things that might have been searchlights, flame-throwers, or boats.

And there was the blood. There were smears of blood high on the funnels. Half-congealed blood lay heel deep in the wrecked foretop, a mushroom-like box stuck up in front of the forward funnel. In that foretop pieces of skull and hair and skin were wedged into battered gun-sights, and it looked as though someone had sloshed buckets of blood on to the walls and ceiling. Below decks, and tucked in odd corners, there were torn clothes, boots, bandages and blankets, all dark and soggy with blood. The salt sea air had not been able to cleanse out the smells of gas, lyddite, cordite and blood.

And the men . . . some of the men crowding her decks yelled and cheered and threw their caps in the air. Some stood quiet, dazed and sightless. Some wept without restraint.

Marine Webb, in *Iris II* recalled, *We didn't expect to see her again at all, after what she'd been through. But she was there ahead of us, looking like a wreck. We were all very tense, from what we'd been through. One man, I don't recall his name now, jumped overboard from our ship on the way back. We couldn't do anything for him.*

Above them all – above Marine Webb (he was 18 then, and a Red Marine), above Captain Carpenter on the shattered cruiser's bridge, the riddled ensigns flew. On the cruiser's quarter-deck there was a horseshoe nailed and there, too, you could read her name: *Vindictive*.

All the ships had just returned from a raid on Zeebrugge. During it, and parallel raids on Ostend, eleven men won the V.C. The blood came from some of the 637 men who suffered wounds or death. It was the first carefully planned commando operation, and it lifted the heart of England at an hour when the land war teetered on the edge of disaster. It was an exploit which a French admiral described as the finest thing done by the Royal Navy, or any other navy, ever.

The Zeebrugge raid took place in hot blood, in indescribable noise and tumult. It was conceived in cold blood, in a quiet room, by anxious men. The men were studying figures set down on a sheet of paper: ... 487,337 ... 333,443 ... 452,063 ... Those were the tonnages of Allied and neutral shipping lost to the German campaign of unrestricted submarine warfare in the closing months of 1917. Earlier in the year Jellicoe, the First Sea Lord, had said that Britain could not survive if such losses continued; and he had welcomed the Passchendaele campaign, with its promise of seizing the Belgian coast, which contained the chief U-boat bases.

The war ground into its fourth bitter winter. Passchendaele ended, and the Army was nearly as far from the Belgian ports as when it began. Jellicoe decided on naval action. He had the man, and the man had a plan. The man was Roger Keyes, then a rear-admiral, and the plan was to block the canals by which the U-boats reached the sea. Jellicoe gave his affirmative decision on Christmas Eve, 1917. On New Year's Day, 1918, Admiral Keyes took over command of the Dover Patrol, and the plan moved into high gear.

So, at 4.53 p.m. April 22, preparations having been completed, a huge fleet steamed east from a meeting point off the Goodwin Sands. Counting co-operating ships to the northward, 140 vessels were engaged. The sole purpose of all of them was to ensure that five old cruisers sailing in the midst of the armada should be sunk at precisely the right times and places to block the canals at Ostend and Zeebrugge. The Ostend operations, exciting and even heroic though they were, are not part of my story, which deals only with the Zeebrugge force, and its block-ships, *Thetis, Intrepid* and *Iphigenia* ...

But I have covered the three and a half months between Keyes's arrival in Dover and the sailing of the fleet in four words, "preparations having been completed". It is necessary to think about those preparations. How, first, do you actually sink a ship exactly across a channel which has a strong current? Ships usually go down bow or stern first, but whichever end goes down first is caught by the current, and swung downstream; the ship would therefore lie along, not athwart, the channel.

Zeebrugge was protected by powerful shore batteries. Therefore the raiders had to be out of range by first light, which, on April 23, would be at 4.30 a.m. A vessel such as *Vindictive* would take 1 hour 50 minutes to get out of range; therefore she had to break off the fight not later than 2.40 a.m. At the beginning, on the other hand, she could not reach Zeebrugge until 1 hour 50 minutes after last light . . .

The fleet would contain ships whose maximum speeds varied from 5 knots to 35 knots; but all had to proceed together for mutual protection, and 9 knots was the slowest that would get them there in time. There had to be ships to carry the extra men for storming parties. There had to be special arrangements to land men on the outside of a heavily defended pier. There had to be ships to prevent attack from enemy destroyers inside Zeebrugge; and others on guard off shore to prevent interference from German forces at sea; and bigger ships farther out to prevent the enemy battle fleet coming down from Heligoland . . . and artificial fog or smoke to enable the block-ships to get past the bristling defences at the harbour mouth . . . and craft to rescue the crews of the block-ships when they had done their work . . . and heavy-gun ships to engage the German shore batteries. . . . All these component parts had to be knitted into a single intricate timetable, iron-strict, but flexible enough so that it could be kept to the minute, rain or shine, wind or fog.

And the ships, and the paramount need for secrecy . . . What ships were to be selected for block-ships? How and where were they to be stripped and filled with concrete? (This one was not too difficult; it was given out that they were being prepared for scrapping.) Ships to carry the storming parties? (Keyes's agents searched every port in the kingdom before they found what they were looking for in the unromantic rotund shapes of two Mersey ferry-boats, *Daffodil* and *Iris II*.)

And, above all, the men, who would make it work or see it fail, according to their guts and skill . . . First Keyes picked his chief staff and captains. Then he called for volunteers, who came from every naval base in the kingdom, and in large numbers from the Grand Fleet. The best were selected from the volunteers. Then those best were trained, carefully and relentlessly, in the exact jobs each would have to perform in the raid. Exact models were made, and rehearsals carried out on them.

And after all that, the enterprise would still be at the mercy of chance. The ships would be steaming, concentrated and in broad daylight for about five hours. During all that time it only needed one enemy U-boat to happen to spot them; one German aircraft to pass over on routine patrol; one Zeppelin or Gotha to see them on its way back from a raid. It would not have taken the Germans long to place a barge or two across the channel entrance, lay some mines, prepare torpedoes and guns, and send a pair of U-boats to sea. Then what was already a hazardous and bloody operation would turn into a holocaust.

By early April all was ready. The fleet waited in its several ports, some at Harwich, some at Dover, some at Dunkirk; and some, the core of the raiders, in an isolated anchorage called the West Swin, a pocket among the shoals 15 miles off the Essex coast. Nothing marked it but the gaunt steel frame of a light beacon. *Iris II* and *Daffodil* and *Vindictive*, all packed with sailors and marines, waited in this mournful spot from April 5 till they finally went. All the month it rained and the wind blew raw. The men in *Vindictive* grew verminous, and there was no place to sleep or eat in comfort until Keyes hurriedly arranged to send the old battleship *Dominion* to the Swin to act as a mother ship. Every night, looking eastward, the sailors saw the livid reflections of heavy gun-flashes on the underside of the distant clouds, and felt the air shake to the rumble of artillery as the British Army fought for its life against the mighty German offensive which had begun on March 21.

Twice weather and other conditions coincided with the desired state of the tide and the moon. Twice the fleet set out. Twice the weather changed and it turned back, once from within a dozen miles of Zeebrugge. On April 22 Keyes again gave the order, *Go!* Again, the ships put to sea . . .

The point of attack was to be Zeebrugge, but the place which was to be throttled by it was Bruges. Bruges (in Flemish Brugge) had once been a port, but the sea had receded and a new port-town (Zee-Brugge, or Sea-Bruges) was created, linked to the old by a canal. Bruges was the U-boat base; there were the shelters, stores, repair machinery, arsenals and all the other elements that kept the boats at sea. Actually to get to sea they went by canal either to Zeebrugge or Ostend.

At Zeebrugge the canal reached the sea inside the shelter of a huge stone mole. It was the largest in the world, a mile and a half long and 100 yds. wide. Railways and a roadway ran out on to the Mole; hangars, warehouses and store-sheds dotted it; at the seaward end there was a lighthouse, a battery of three 5.9-in. guns and six 4.1-in. guns. The Mole, the entrance to the canal, the gun positions, and many individual buildings were defended by machine-gun posts, barbed-wire entanglements and concrete pill-boxes. The concrete of the Mole was interrupted near its shoreward end by a section of steel viaduct. This allowed the tide to run freely back and forth, and so prevented the inside of the harbour from silting up.

Keyes's object was to sink three block-ships in the canal. To be sure that they got there, they had to be helped. First, there was the necessity of engaging the German guns on the Mole. Otherwise, at that range of a hundred yards or so, the guns could blow the block-ships out of the water before they reached the

*Sir Doveton Sturdee, victor at the Falkland Islands, and
Roger Keyes, who planned the Zeebrugge raid*

Vindictive *after Zeebrugge*

canal. This was the job of *Vindictive*, assisted by *Daffodil* and *Iris II*. She was to lay herself alongside the outside of the Mole right opposite the gun batteries, and land her assaulting marines and sailors, with flame-throwers and heavy mortars, literally on top of the guns.

Next, the Germans must be prevented from rushing reinforcements on to and along the Mole, who might retake the guns, or even fight their way on to *Vindictive*. This was the task of two old submarines C 1 and C 3. They were filled with explosive, and their job was to ram themselves under the viaduct section of the Mole, and there blow themselves up, destroying the viaduct. They were fitted with an automatic steering device to enable the captain and his skeleton crew to get off before sending the vessels the last few hundred yards on their own; but neither skipper deigned to use it. They wanted to make sure . . . There was a light motor skiff on each submarine for the final getaway.

Finally, when German attention was thoroughly concentrated on *Vindictive* and the broken viaduct; when the Mole guns would be out of action – then the block-ships were to steam in, pass down the length of the outer harbour, and sink themselves in the canal entrance.

A thousand details filled in and rounded out this essentially simple plan. Wing-Commander Brock, of the fireworks firm, invented and perfected devices to make large amounts of artificial smoke. Coastal Motor Boats (C.M.B.s) were to go in first, and lay down clouds of this smoke, to prevent the Germans seeing the approach of the bigger ships. Other C.M.B.s were to follow the block-ships up the harbour and take off survivors when they had scuttled themselves. Monitors at sea were to bombard the emplaced shore guns. Two thousand men would be doing two thousand different but closely interlocked jobs, all as a projection of the will of one man. He would be there, lying to sea off the Mole in the dark and the fog, his flag above him in the destroyer *Warwick*. Keyes, the nearest thing to Nelson since Nelson, would have given an arm and an eye to lead the assault in person, but with all the other responsibilities on him he dared not.

The ships steamed on. Many of the very small, very slow craft were under tow. Night fell.

The monitors opened fire with their heavy guns on the German shore batteries at 11.20 p.m. At 11.40 the C.M.B.s roared out of the night and started weaving back and forth across the end of the Mole, making dense clouds of smoke. The Germans fired star-shell. Everyone who was there has commented on the extraordinary effect this produced as seen from the approaching British ships. The shells burst brilliantly above the low, dark fog, then fell into it, and from blazing stars became vague glowing nebulae, hung about with twisting, fiery vapour.

The wind changed, blowing more from southerly, and thinning the smoke. At

11.56 *Vindictive* burst out of the black, flaming fog. The end of the Mole lay 300 yds. away on her port bow. *Daffodil* and *Iris II* wallowed after. Instantly the German batteries opened a vicious fire at point blank range. *Vindictive* answered with all her guns. Captain Carpenter put her alongside the Mole at 1 minute past midnight, 1 minute behind schedule.

Now the problem was to keep her there, and get the landing gangways on to the Mole. (These were hardly more than hinged ladders.) A big swell heaved the old cruiser up and down the side of the high wall, the grapnels would not grip the parapet properly. German shells kept smashing into the ship and the two ferry-boats. One burst in a flat where fifty-six marines were waiting to go ashore, and killed forty-nine of them; another burst in the wardroom, killing thirty more. A 3-knot tide pushed the ship away from the Mole as the swell heaved her up and down. Carpenter ordered *Daffodil* to push *Vindictive* against the Mole, and hold her there. This the gallant little vessel at once did, her engines working full blast.

The three senior commanders of the storming party were killed. *Iris II* worked in front of *Vindictive*, and for long minutes tried to hold her grapnels to the Mole. Officer after officer gave his life here, being shot, blown to bits, falling into the trough between ship and Mole, to be crushed and drowned. *Iris II* pulled out and began to land her men across *Vindictive*. By then *Vindictive* had put two gangways on to the parapet and her bluejackets (wearing army khaki) were running ashore across them – 30 ft. up, without hand rails, in a hell of fire, with the ship rising and falling 10 ft. In the stern cabin an employee of Brocks, who had never been to sea before, fired rockets out of a scuttle to light up the end of the Mole, as a guide to the incoming block-ships.

Closer to shore, the submarine C 1's engine had failed. C 3 ran on alone, surfaced, at $9\frac{1}{2}$ knots towards the viaduct section of the Mole. Germans on the Mole spotted her, held her for a moment in searchlight glare, and opened heavy fire. Then the firing died down and the searchlight went out. Apparently the Germans decided that the submarine was trying to get through the viaduct pilings, which they knew was impossible. They knew she'd hang herself up on them, and be captured. At 12.15 Lieutenant Sandford ran C 3 hard into the cross members of the viaduct. She rode in as far as her conning tower, before grinding to a stop.

Let Stoker Bindall, one of the six men on board, tell the story . . . *We lowered the skiff and stood by while the commander touched off the fuse* (remember they were directly under the Mole road and railway, occupied at this time by numerous armed Germans) . . . *then we tumbled into the skiff and pushed off. We had rather a bit of bad luck. The propeller fouled the exhaust pipe and left us with only a couple of oars, and two minutes to get away.*

Bullets began to strike. Bindall was hit twice, the coxswain was hit, and another sailor. Only the rise and fall of the cockleshell on the waves, making it a difficult target, saved them. At 12.20 a tremendous explosion blasted the C 3, the viaduct, the roadway, the rails – and all the Germans who had been standing there – 200 ft. into the air. The raiders set up a great cheer – the men on the *Vindictive*, those struggling to get ashore, those already on the Mole.

It was now that the human bone and hair became wedged into the gun-sights in *Vindictive*'s foretop. A shell burst in the tiny space, killing every man except one. *We all went down in a bunch,* Sergeant Finch said, *and I had a job to get out from underneath . . . I don't really know what I did.* We know, though: Finch worked the gun alone until he fainted from his own wounds. He was one of the Zeebrugge V.C.s.

The marines and bluejackets storming the Mole had little luck. *Vindictive* had come alongside 400 yds. too close to shore. Instead of landing on top of the German guns the stormers had to fight their way towards them, along the flat concrete, through the barbed-wire, raked by machine-guns. No amount of heroism, and there was plenty, could do it. In the confused fighting England lost a brave man and great inventor, Brock. He went into a captured look-out post to examine a German range-finder and was never reliably seen again.

His requiem was, appropriately, a Brock's Benefit . . . The noise shattered the ear drums. Rockets, machine-guns, rifles, grenades, star-shells, mortars, and guns of every calibre were exploding at full blast. The destroyer *North Star* and dozens of small craft tore about the harbour making smoke and firing guns and torpedoes. *North Star* was shattered by the Mole batteries, and sank. Marines tossed grenades at German destroyers moored alongside the Mole . . .

. . . At 12.25 *Thetis* passed the end of the Mole, going at full speed, closely followed by *Intrepid* and *Iphigenia*, each attended by a C.M.B. Each block-ship was supposed to have only fifty men aboard, just enough to work the ship into position, and sink it. The rest of the crews had been transferred to other ships 20 miles out. Or should have been! But there had been a sort of mutiny, and the extra men had refused or evaded their orders, and stayed aboard to see the fight . . .

Commander Sneyd, in *Thetis*, saw what he hoped was a way past the harbour floating defences, but he fouled the nets and ran his ship aground just to one side of the dredged channel, well outside the canal mouth. He signalled the others to pass him to starboard. They did so – (*Iphigenia* rammed a barge in the process, and pushed it into the canal mouth ahead of her) – and got into position under a storm of close-range fire. By using rudder and reverse engines against the strong thrust of the current, the young skippers sank their ships exactly across the canal.

The C.M.B. 110, one of the escorts, had already been sunk, so Lieutenant Dean of C.M.B. 282 had to pick up the crews of two block-ships – some eighty men instead of fifty on each; and all under the close, murderous fire. Then Dean found a cutter from *Iphigenia*, with more men aboard, and took it in tow from his bow, and left Zeebrugge harbour at full speed, backwards, towing the cutter and carrying nearly 200 men instead of his normal complement of a dozen.

Now Captain Carpenter in *Vindictive* saw that the block-ships had reached the canal. The job was done, and he ordered *Daffodil* to give the recall blasts on her siren. (*Vindictive*'s own searchlight and siren were gone.) In twos and threes, in sixes and sevens, carrying their wounded and their dead, the men came back. At 1.10 a.m. *Vindictive* swung hard a-starboard and broke clear, with *Daffodil* and *Iris II*, all going as fast as their battered condition would allow. Behind them the little C.M.B.s weaved and wound, making smoke to protect them from the shore batteries. The covering destroyers were taking such violent evasive action that in one of them, H.M.S. *Broke*, Petty Officer Davey recorded that the bridge gave twenty-eight orders on the engine-room telegraph in one minute.

Sergeant Wright, of the Royal Marine Light Infantry, had taken a most gallant part in the raid, leading one of the storming platoons. He was not on any of the ships that returned towards England. He and eleven other marines were on the Mole. They watched the ships go with concern, but not alarm – yet. They understood that C.M.B.s would be hanging about for some time yet, to pick up stragglers. No C.M.B.s came; only, at 3 a.m., a German officer and fifty soldiers. The helpless marines, lost through one of the sad, inevitable accidents of war, passed into captivity.

Out to sea, the fleet began to reform. In the earliest hours of St George's Day the ships hurried through the torn shoal waters towards Dover. They had blocked the Zeebrugge Canal, which was a great feat. They had pioneered a planned commando raid, which was more. They had relit the fire in Nelson's Navy, which was more again. Most of all, they had made every Briton stand up straighter in face of the world.

Submarines on the surface

Take-off from a platform fitted to the gun turret of a warship

Parachute descent from a kite balloon

A wireless transmitting station

A flame-thrower in action

An air camera

Gas sentry, masked, ringing an alarm

An Austrian helicopter: 1915-16

An aircraft carrier dazzle-painted for camouflage

Lloyd George, became Prime Minister in 1916

*Two V.C.s: Sergeant Whittle and
Corporal Howell*

An airship carries, then releases, a Sopwith Camel scout

Tank crossing a British trench prior to attacking

130

Rehearsal for a Christmas pantomime at the front

Revolution takes Russia out of the war:
soldiers in Petrograd with red flags fixed
to their bayonets

The United States enters the war

"Black Jack" Pershing, commander of the American Expeditionary Force in France (by courtesy of Radio Times Hulton Picture Library)

HIS GRACE AND THE THIRSTY SAILORS

This is another land-and-sea story, which actually took place earlier in the war. It's a timeless sort of tale, though, and in atmosphere fits in much better with Zeebrugge than with Mons or Coronel.

It began on Guy Fawkes' Day, 1915, when the German submarine U. 35 torpedoed H.M.S. *Tara* off the north coast of Africa. *Tara* was not a real man-o'-war. In peacetime she used to run between Holyhead and Kingston, carrying passengers and the Irish Mail for the London and North Western Railway. On the outbreak of war she went into the Navy, complete with her crew of Welshmen, as an auxiliary armed merchant-cruiser. The Admiralty put a Royal Navy captain in over-all command of her, but had the sense to choose another Welshman for the job – Captain H. Gwatkin Williams, R.N.

In the sinking ninety-two men were saved, twelve lost. U. 35 towed the survivors to land in the ships' boats, and there handed them over to the Turks. Her captain must have known that the prisoners would have a hard time ashore, because he offered to take Captain Gwatkin Williams aboard the submarine, and hand him over to proper Turkish authority in Turkey itself, as a gesture due from one naval officer to another. Gwatkin Williams, however, very rightly stayed with his crew.

There were only two or three Turks in the local garrison, and they were ignorant, brutal and bored. The prisoners were really in the hands of the wild Senussi tribesmen, at that time risen in holy *jehad* against the British. The sailors were kept for days in a rocky ravine, without shade or rest, the tribesmen squatting all round with guns, threatening to massacre them. Then the Senussi gave out Arab clothes and forced the party to march into the interior.

It was a hell march, alternately bitter cold and burning hot. There was never enough to eat and when the meat gave out there was only a half ration of rice, with tea and sugar – that's all. On Christmas Day they invented Petty Officer's Pudding: it was made of flour scrounged from the Turkish guards, kneaded with boiled rice and hoarded sugar, the whole boiled for five hours in the Master's trousers. They ate snails and were eaten by fleas. They started to die, the first man on November 13 . . . the next on January 5, another on the 10th, another on the 28th, another on February 19 – all from cold, starvation and dysentery.

One of the Duke of Westminster's
Armoured Cars

136

Now Captain Gwatkin Williams did something which was to decide their fate. He wrote a strong letter to the Turkish commander in Libya (whoever he might be), protesting against the inhuman treatment he and his men were receiving. The bullying Turkish captain now in charge of them sent the letter on, laughing to himself. That, he knew, would be the last ever heard of *that!*

But far to the east, wheels were turning – both figuratively and literally. The Duke of Westminster had presented the nation with a regiment of armoured cars, which he himself commanded. Not long afterwards, in the aftermath of a successful attack on a Turk-Senussi force in the desert, a mass of letters was discovered in the Turkish commander's tent. One of them, written from El Hakkim, was Captain Gwatkin Williams's protest. This was the first news of the *Tara*'s crew since the torpedoing.

The Duke sprang to action. He found a man who said he had been to El Hakkim (he thought), with his father, thirty years before. It was *that* way (he thought) about 120 miles off (maybe). Did he have a recollection of a low hill, and a single date palm on it?

At 3 in the afternoon of St Patrick's Day, 1916, one of the dejected, exhausted sailors thought he saw a car coming across the desert. The others first scoffed; then, with wild and mounting excitement, believed. The cars swept on. Moments later they roared into the camp and opened fire, killing the Turkish and Senussi guards and a few innocent villagers. Half an hour later, the surviving sailors safe in the ambulances, His Grace gave the order and the force headed east for Sollum, the sea, hot baths and square meals.

At a dinner given in the crew's honour by the London and North Western Railway, Captain Gwatkin Williams's cloakroom ticket number was U. 35. A little later, strolling along Bow Street in the semi-blackout, about 10 p.m. of a May night, he walked into a camel.

Balkan front

138

J UNE 1918: *No one can get any meat or butter or bacon or poultry without present-ing in exchange an absurd little paper coupon . . . In years to come people will hardly believe that such things really* were . . .

Mrs Bilbrough could not be expected to guess that our difficulty would not lie in believing about the ration coupons, but in believing there was ever a time when people should think them – or air raids – or War Bonds – so extraordinary. But Mrs Bilbrough was obviously an optimist and at the time she wrote it would have required a very cynical mind to foresee, or accept, even if the matter were to have been irrefutably demonstrated, that the travail through which England and the world were passing was not the end, only the beginning.

At the time of that quotation, the end of the war was in sight. The German Army launched a great offensive against the British on March 21, 1918, achieving instant and huge success. So serious was the situation that funk at last forced the Allies to take a step which common sense had never succeeded in doing: the appointment of a supreme commander. The French general, Foch, was chosen. By the exercise of iron nerve, and through the stubborn fighting of the soldiers, Foch finally held the German offensive only a few miles outside Paris.

Now the German Army really was in the condition that Haig had wishfully proclaimed it to be in nine months earlier – spent, sullen, at last convinced that it could not win. The man responsible for this state of affairs was the same Ludendorff whose military genius had planned the offensive. There are many who believe that Ludendorff should have accepted in 1917 that it had become impossible to break the Allied armies. If he had continued to fight on the defensive, as throughout Passchendaele, punishing each attack with heavy but limited counter-strokes, it is likely that the Allied armies would have lost their confidence. It is doubtful, indeed, whether after Passchendaele the British Army *would* have attacked, for long, or with any determination. The French were still recovering from the Chemin des Dames and the mutinies, and the Italians from Caporetto. That would have left the offensive entirely to the raw Americans, who couldn't arrive in large enough numbers until late 1918 or 1919. It is not hard to imagine what kind of an outcry would have been raised in the United States, and it is hardly possible that such attacks could have succeeded even if they were mounted.

Ahead, therefore, the Allied governments would have seen not victory but further dissension, further hopeless bloodshed. A negotiated peace, which was desired by many important people on both sides and among the neutrals, would have resulted.

But it was the Germans who assaulted, throwing their all into the scales. On our side, soldiers too discouraged to attack were yet men enough to fight in their own defence. When the offensive was finally held, it was the Germans, now physically the weaker, who had to suffer the inevitable counter-blow. To them it came on August 8, and they could not take it. The war would last some more months, more shells would be fired, more of the world's resources in material and manpower would be carefully destroyed, but these were no more than the noisy running down of a wound-up machine. As a contest, the war was over.

In East Africa the brilliant and gallant von Lettow Vorbeck evaded defeat and capture to the end, and carried his arms back to Germany. On most other fronts the collapse of Germany's will was immediately detected by her local associates, their commanders, and troops. They, too, gave up, while still outwardly fighting on. The natural result, everywhere, was a final crushing Allied victory. In Italy Vittorio Veneto overlaid the bitter memory of Caporetto. In Mesopotamia Sharqat evened the score for Kut. From Salonika Franchet d'Esperey swept like a scythe through Bulgaria, Serbia and Rumania. In Palestine the campaign came to a climax in the victory of Armageddon, which I shall describe in some detail later, because it was such a classic campaign, the one flawless piece of British generalship throughout the war.

By the Armistice, the Air Age had been born. Heavy bombers looked like heavy bombers now, the scouting planes looked like aircraft rather than kites ridden by Supermen, long woollen underwear and all. The wrecked Zeppelins are not monstrous piles of Meccano but recognizably crashes of big aircraft such as we see in the papers. The concept of air war had been understood, and put into practice, and had immeasurably advanced the concept of the air as a new element in man's peacetime existence. One of the fathers of the Air Age was "Boom" Trenchard, creator first of the Independent bombing force, and later of the Royal Air Force, the first in the world to be independent of the older land- or sea-based services, the first to develop a distinctive "air outlook".

Aeroplanes flew, tanks rumbled, but in peace and war it was still a world of animals. In the calculations of the supply and transport services, fodder continued to occupy as large a place as shells. Veterinary surgeons were as necessary as doctors, and a great deal more necessary than mechanics to the success of the average operation. In the Great War, millions of animals worked, suffered and died with the humans. The difference, that the humans knew what they were fighting for, was in many cases quite illusory.

But it was, after all, a war of people. Wherever there are people, there will be courage as well as cowardice, humour as well as misery, love as well as hate. Our photographs show a tiny handful of the faces of the Great War. Look at them, and accept our brotherhood with them. They were the forerunners. In their place, we could not have done better, if as well.

Air raid damage in London

Children sorting out salvage,
Buckinghamshire

Faces of the Great War

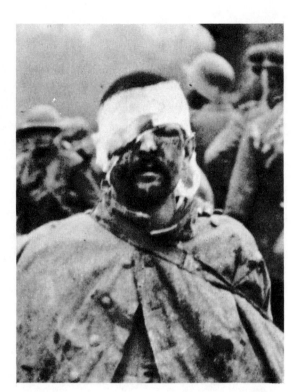

Faces of the Great War

Faces of the Great War

Faces of the Great War

British infantry marching over the Jebel Hamrin, Mesopotamia

German infantry advancing in 1918 offensive

Italian front

147

Foch

Allenby

Ludendorff (by courtesy of Radio Times Hulton Picture Library)

Queen Mary with "Boom" Trenchard

African Scouts

*Major-General Dunsterville (the original of Kipling's Stalky)
commanded a British mission to Armenia: known as the Dunsterforce*

South Persia: officers and men are from the Indian 15th Lancers, the rock carving shows the capture of the Roman Emperor Valerian by Shapur

Officers and S.E.5A Scouts of No. 1 Squadron

Bristol F.2.B. fighter

Wreckage of a Zeppelin brought down over England

Handley Page heavy bomber: *Type L/400*

Carrier pigeon, shot in the left eye while carrying a message across the North Sea

Donkeys used for transport in the desert

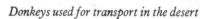

Machine-gun carts drawn by dogs

154

Mules bringing supplies to the front

Oxen used to transport shells, Balkan front

The Imperial Camel Corps Brigade

Mesopotamia: German heavy artillery
moving forward
(by courtesy of Ullstein)

Church parade, before going into the trenches

ARMAGEDDON

At first, in the warm darkness, there was nothing to see. Sounds to hear, yes – the clatter and crunch of hoofs on a loose, rough surface; the clink of steel on stone; the creak of saddlery; the jingle of bits and rumble of gun-wheels; the stertorous breathing of tired horses and tired riders.

And there were smells – the acid sweat of men and animals, the sharp tang of oiled leather.

And there was taste – in the mouth, in the air, on the teeth, the taste of dust.

And now the eye, becoming accustomed to the blackness, began to see golden sparks, like fireflies, streaking briefly from the horseshoes; and the glimmer of an officer's torch as he peered down at a folded map; and the dim arch of his horse's neck as it plodded on, head down.

In the first faint swell of dawn, points of light began to appear twelve feet up in the air, at first a dull grey, steel sheen, then a myriad twinkle, at last a river of light and colour, a thousand lance points, a thousand red and white pennants. Now the morning showed the khaki turbans wound round the men's heads, and the brown faces and the hawk noses and slim hands. Black beards passed, curled moustaches, dark eyes hooded with fatigue – suddenly the blue eyes of a British subaltern – on all the rime of dust, all shoulders slumped. The steel tide moved on into the north.

So passed the 4th Indian Cavalry Division, spearhead of the British armies in Palestine; and at the point of all, the 2nd Bengal Lancers. It was September 20, 1918. The pass they rode up is called the Musmus Pass. It is broad at first, a shallow stony waste inclining towards a low crest-line. At the top it narrows. When the Pharaoh Thothmes III took his army through 3,377 years earlier, his foot-soldiers had to go in single file there. On the north side the Pharaoh defeated the Syrians at the battle of Megiddo, on the edge of the Plain of Esdraelon; which has another name, a name that has come to signify all war and strife: Armageddon.

The Musmus Pass had been widened since Thothmes's time, but it was still a dangerous, tight place. The 2nd Lancers did not linger there. After a brief rest they rode on down towards Armageddon. Mt. Tabor and the hills of Nazareth stood up clear against the growing light. A dawn mist obscured the plain and the regiment's particular objective, the town and railway station of El Afuleh; but the C.O. took a compass bearing and they rode on confidently down the ill-defined track.

At 5.30 a.m. the leading riders came under heavy rifle and machine-gun fire from directly in front. Captain Davison, commanding in the absence of more senior officers sick and wounded, rode forward and found that the enemy, Turkish infantry, were holding a position half a mile ahead. He thought back to the events of the night. At 3 o'clock, when near the crest of the pass, they'd come upon 100 Turks sitting round a camp fire, their arms piled. The Turks had surrendered without a struggle, dumbfounded at the apparition of Indian lancers so far behind the front. Davison guessed that those men must have been the advanced guard of an infantry battalion. Now he had come upon the main body of that battalion.

While the leading troop, under the Rissaldar Major, held the Turks frontally, Davison got out his binoculars and took a quick look at the ground and the enemy position. He was sure he could see the Turkish flanks. The ground seemed to be open and clear of obstacles. The earth was heavy black cotton soil, but not too heavy to prevent horses galloping. Davison called up his "D" Squadron commander, Captain Vaughan, and ordered him to sweep right, wheel, and charge the enemy from that flank.

Vaughan put his squadron into a trot and moved off. Next in the order of march came Captain Whitworth and "B" Squadron. Whitworth had heard the firing and seen the enemy, and now saw the outward swing of "D" Squadron.

These were Bengal Lancers, trained in polo field and Frontier scrap to act fast, act bold. Whitworth didn't wait for orders. He didn't even ride forward to get them. He too wheeled his squadron right and moved them at a fast trot outside the right wing of "D". Hear him now: . . . *Bullets were coming unpleasantly close . . . I increased the pace to a hand gallop and edged toward the right . . . Just then (we) ran into a wire fence hidden in the jowar (a crop) which covered that part of the plain. I was on ahead and left it to Rissaldar Jang Bahadur Singh to reform the squadron . . . Bullets were coming thick and fast and I imagined that the squadron had had pretty heavy casualties . . . I was in a blue funk of striking an uncrossable nullah (ravine) . . . We were moving at a good 15 miles an hour by now. . . . It was just then that I caught sight of the Turks. . . . (My men) all saw red and broke into a hell for leather gallop. Before I realized it we were right on top of the enemy, and it was only when I saw a young Turk deliberately aiming at me that I realized I was still holding my map in my right hand and had forgotten to draw my sword. The little brute missed me and ran under my horse's neck and tried to jab his rifle in my stomach. I had just time to draw and thrust over my left knee. The point got him somewhere in the neck and he went down like a house of cards . . . I made for (a Turk) who had murderous intentions but changed his mind at the last moment. My point caught him plumb between the shoulders and nearly dislocated my arm. . . . I remember my orderly, Lal Chand, on my second horse, Advocate, who had the regimental flag furled round his lance, dragging along the ground a Turk who had stuck on the point . . . I saw Jemadar Gobind Singh, v.c. deliver a magnificent cut at an opponent . . .*

And Captain Vaughan: *. . . I have never enjoyed any time of my life as much as that week . . . On the morning of September 20th, after a charge outside El Afuleh, having settled down to a Boche cigar and a bottle of ditto hock I would not have changed places with President Wilson himself.*

Well he might feel on top of the world! The regiment had killed fifty Turks with the lance, and captured 470, at a total cost of one man wounded and ten horses that had to be destroyed.

A score of squadron commanders could have written something like that narrative. Back on the Western Front men were dying in thousands as the Allied armies smashed grimly into the Hindenburg Line, but in this grand and sweeping Palestine victory even colonels and generals had a sort of boyish fun.

Palestine was then a part of the ramshackle Turkish empire, though peopled mainly by Arabs, who wanted to be free under their own rulers. When Turkey came into the war on the German side, Britain's first task was to prevent the Turks advancing from Palestine from capturing or cutting the Suez Canal. This achieved, defence changed to attack – with indifferent success until a new commander was sent out in June 1917 to revive the dispirited Army. That general was Sir Edmund Allenby.

Within six months he had carried out Lloyd George's politically motivated request to give him Jerusalem "as a Christmas present for the British nation". Now, after nearly nine months of stalemate, Allenby planned to attack again; but not to capture more ground, or seize more cities, however famous. His aim was the classic and proper one of a great general: to destroy the Turkish Army.

As the clocks tick off the inexorable minutes towards zero hour, let us look at the scene, the actors, the crowding extras . . . The German general, Liman von Sanders, in chief command of all enemy forces, was a man of skill but not genius, a man who would hold fast to what he had, rather than manoeuvre, a man of determination. Allenby intended to use this very quality against him. Allenby was not one man but two: a huge, strong soldier with the traditional general's choleric face . . . and a subtle eye for beauty; a man who could notice the slimness of Feisal's hands, and the delicacy of tint in a song-bird's wing; a man who screamed in apoplectic fury when he saw Australians riding in shorts or Yeomanry without their chinstraps down; and who detected and managed the touchy genius in Lawrence; Allenby, whom every soldier in the Army knew as The Bull; Allenby, who wrote to his wife . . . *of birds, there are larks, wheatears, shrikes, bee-eaters, hawks, vultures. There is a merry bird, the rufous warbler, who haunts the locality. He is pert and friendly. Looks like a big nightingale, has the manners of a robin, and flirts his tail like a redstart . . .*

The enemy were mainly Turks, with a small number of Germans. The Turk had up to this point shown himself a formidable soldier, particularly in defence. Stubborn, brave, inured to the diseases, the climate and the starvation rations, imbued with an obstinate self-respect, he was a hard man to beat. But some recent actions indicated that he had had enough of this war. He had begun to see that it was not being fought for any conceivable benefit to Turkey, and he was no longer willing to die for it.

The few Germans were invariably brave, skilful and well led. The Arabs conscripted into the Turkish Army were all waiting an opportunity to desert.

There were Arabs on the Allied side too – the formless, undisciplined Bedouin of Lawrence and Feisal. For the rest, Allenby commanded cavalrymen from Australia and New Zealand, Yeomanry and line infantry from Great Britain, West Indians and Jews. The bulk of his force, both in infantry and cavalry was of the Indian Army. There were Sikhs and Mahrattas, Punjabis and Dogras, Pathans and Gurkhas. Some of this motley, many-tongued crew were seasoned veterans, some were new to the theatre and to war; but all were imbued with an enormous confidence. The Allies were winning the war, and everyone knew it. Allenby had already shown that he would win the battles.

The land . . . it is a harsh, bare land, except on the extreme west, where oranges and cotton and grain crops grow in the coastal plain. Allenby's Army stood on an east-west line 50 miles long. The left rested on the Mediterranean, the centre bestrode the Judaean Hills north of Jerusalem, and the right, the east, scorched in the Jordan valley. Lawrence's Arabs dominated the desert farther east again. Allenby's eyes saw, his intelligence moulded, his will determined . . . One evening he called his subordinate generals and gave his orders. The Army would hold on the right, advance on the left, wheel inwards, and destroy the Turks.

The battle would resemble the opening of a door. The front line was the door, its hinge to the right (the Jordan). Just as one opens a door by grasping the handle, at the other end from the hinge, and pushing – so Allenby's infantry would push along the coastal plain. Once the door had been forced a little open, the cavalry would pass through, riding wide and deep, and at last wheel right to entrap all those, by now far behind, still trying to hold the door shut. Liman von Sanders was a man who would obstinately try to hold the door long after it was too late.

This being Allenby's plan, his first task was to convince the Turks of the opposite, i.e. that he intended to hold on the coast and strike up or across the Jordan. The back-room boys had a fine time. They took over hotels, summarily threw out the clients, and urgently prepared the hotel for use as a military command post. They moved Corps headquarters from one end of the front to the other, but left wireless stations behind, in operation, with the usual stack of messages to send, so that enemy monitors would detect no change. They pitched new camps in the Jordan valley and detailed troops to march up openly by day, back secretly by night, up again the next day . . . and again, and again. Lawrence spread the word that forage would be required for large numbers of cavalry in Amman, far east of the Jordan. Above all, Allenby actually kept a considerable force in the Jordan valley all through the worst of the summer heat. Liman and his staff assured themselves that no one would dare to keep troops, especially the proverbially "difficult" Australians, in such a place without real and sound cause.

Steadily, quietly, the preparations went on. The weight of the infantry moved imperceptibly, by night, towards the western end of the front. The rest spread themselves out so that there should be no visible gaps or weak places. By D minus 1 five divisions of infantry, some 90,000 men, stood ready along the westernmost 15 miles of the front. Behind them, hidden in the orange groves, were the horses and the men and the wheeled guns, the armoured cars, the lances and swords and carbines, of three full divisions of cavalry – the 4th Indian, 5th Indian and Australian Mounted. In the Indian divisions roughly one man out of three was British. The British mounted regiments were all Yeomanry.

D-Day was set for September 18. Outwardly everyone was calm, from the burly commander-in-chief, out bird-watching, to the Gurkhas serenely playing cards under the orange trees. The tension was there, though. The Army waited, taut and ready.

On September 17 an Indian havildar (sergeant) deserted to the Turks. We know *now* that he told the enemy the British attack would come along the coast. *Then*, no one knew what he had told, or even how much he knew. In any case, would Liman believe him? Might he think it was a double bluff? How could the havildar, or Liman, be sure that the coastal attack was to be the main one?

British headquarters spent an agonizing thirty-six hours, wondering. Actually, Liman decided that he had no time to act even if the havildar's information were correct. If he tried to move his troops at this last moment, in the poor condition of the roads and railways behind him, the battle would probably begin with half his men on the move and unable to take part at all. True, too, to his character, Liman decided to stand and fight.

At 4 a.m. on September 18 the masses of cavalry began to move out of the orange groves. The columns advanced at a walk towards the hidden front. At 4.30, before the cavalry had reached their positions, 384 guns opened the artillery preparation. At once the rockets started flaring up as the Turks signalled for help from their own guns. Allenby's infantry went over the top.

Leading on the extreme left, actually on the beach and just in from it, went the best known regiment in the Indian Army – the Guides. In a short, bloody fight they took their objective, and 600 prisoners. Over 400 men of the Guides shed their blood upon that field where, close by and 700 years earlier, Richard Coeur de Lion defeated Saladin.

The door began to open. A little to the east a young captain of Rajputana Rifles, with six men, captured three guns of an enemy battery. The fourth gun the Turks had hooked in and driven away; but the captain leaped on to a captured horse and galloped after them alone, and turned them back to surrender. (The captain's name was Pete Rees, a soft-voiced 5 ft. 2 in. Welshman, who became a major-general in Hitler's War, and took Mandalay, and was called the Green Gremlin, and was my own commander and friend.)

Wider opened the door – wide enough. The cavalry went through. Hodson's Horse passed their comrades of the Guides Infantry, and rode on along the beach so fast that the divisional commander, who thought that they would founder their horses, couldn't catch them to tell them to slow down. Farther right the 4th Division went through, and the 2nd Lancers, and the young captains Davison and Whitworth and Vaughan, and Jemadar Gobind Singh, v.c., who was to deliver that tremendous cut at El Afuleh. (The 2nd Lancers came to Palestine after almost three years in France. Gobind Singh won his V.C. at Cambrai in 1917. Three times in a single morning he volunteered to carry vital messages through the German machine-gun and artillery barrage. Three times his horse was killed under him – the last time cut in half by a direct shell hit behind the saddle. Three times Gobind Singh finally delivered the message, running and crawling on under murderous fire.)

Historically, there is not much more to say. Armageddon was one battle that went according to plan. While the Turkish infantry fought grimly against a more powerful, more numerous, and more determined British Army, Allenby's cavalry swept ever farther and deeper into their rear. Liman von Sanders himself was all but captured. Division, Corps and Army headquarters vanished under the fast moving waves of horsemen. The 2nd Lancers covered 80 miles in the first thirty-two hours, including the fight at El Afuleh and two other scraps.

The door swung wide, with a crash that shook it clear off its hinges. Defeat turned into flight, flight into rout. The scenes covered the gamut of war.

There was grimness . . . In the Barada gorge outside Damascus (the Barada is Naaman's River Abana), thousands of Turks were bottled up, unable to move in either direction, and the Australians held the heights. The firing and slashing went on until the Abana ran red with blood and in the narrow gorge a man could hardly find his way through the smashed carts, overturned guns, shattered horses, and bleeding, screaming men.

There was panache a-plenty, with the prize going to Rissaldar Nur Ahmed of Hodson's Horse, who rode at 300 Turks with only his orderly for company. He fired one shot; then the 300 Turks surrendered.

There was humour. Our Captain Whitworth reports the antics of a R.A.F. biplane . . . *first it dropped a bomb on one of the Dorsetshire Yeomanry picquets not far from us . . . Not wishing the same thing to happen to us we began waving the aeroplane flags and showing the white aircraft strips . . . the aeroplane flew over the same picquet . . . and dropped a message to say that a large force of Turks was close to them and that it would fly over the position and fire a red light there. It flew over us, and fired its light; then made off, to the unbounded joy of the Dorsets and ourselves.*

There was horror, above all where Turk and Arab inflicted on each other the utmost barbarities thinkable by men full of hate, men who felt betrayed, men who had inherited and grown up with a harsh disregard for human life and suffering. Lawrence has a terrible description of the scene at Tafas, a village where the retreating Turks murdered the old men, bashed in children's heads, and left women upside down over hurdles, naked, bayonetted between the legs. At Deraa Station a few hours later the Arabs did as much to the Turks, for hours looting, burning and torturing in a frenzy of hate and destruction. All this is shown in David Lean's brilliant film, *Lawrence of Arabia*.

Damascus fell, then Beirut, then Aleppo. October came and passed, and the campaign at last ended, Allenby's men had taken 75,000 prisoners and 360 guns. The number of enemy dead and wounded is unknown and uncountable. We suffered just 5,666 casualties of all kinds, of which 1,200 were killed or missing. The cavalry lost barely 100 men.

On October 30 the Sultan's representative signed an armistice aboard Admiral Gough-Calthorpe's battleship *Agamemnon*. The war against Turkey was over. The regiments passed from Armageddon, with a sigh, to the first bivouacs of peace – among the muscatel vineyards, beside the blue Mediterranean, under arches that had seen the passing of Roman legions, Turkish janissaries and Napoleonic *chasseurs*. In the Middle East the war was over. The more dangerous, hate-laden years of a surface peace had begun.

9th Hodson's Horse

The Advance to Damascus: Indian Lancers

Sherifian troops in Damascus

Sandbag defences on the Mediterranean near Arsuf

Turkish prisoners (by courtesy of Ullstein)

November 11, 1918: *I was trying to write a coherent letter this morning when all of a sudden the air was rent by a tremendous* Bang ! ! *My instant thought was – a* raid! . . . *But when another great explosion shook the windows and the hooters at Woolwich began to scream like things demented, and the guns started frantically firing all round us like an all mighty fugue* (!) *I knew that this was no raid, but that the signing of the armistice had been* accomplished! *Signal upon signal took up the news; the glorious pulverising news – that the end had come at last, and* the greatest war in history was over.